The Amazon Way on IoT

10 Principles for Every Leader from the World's Leading Internet of Things Strategies

John Rossman

Table of Contents

Prologue: Connect the Dots

As to methods there may be a million and then some, but principles are few. The man who grasps principles can successfully select his own methods. The man who tries methods, ignoring principles, is sure to have trouble.

—HARRINGTON EMERSON, RENOWNED EFFICIENCY ENGINEER AND BUSINESS THEORIST

You've likely purchased this book (thank you very much) because you've read the headlines about how the Internet of Things, or IoT, will transform business and society. Or perhaps you are curious about the world's most powerful retailer, Amazon, and how it is approaching the heralded technologies and strategies behind IoT.

The Internet of Things is in its early days, truly "Day 1." Land grabs are being made by many companies trying to establish strategic positions, including Amazon, Microsoft, IBM, Google, and General Electric. Lots of devices are being connected. Some devices make sense and add value to the customer, and many more are either poorly conceived or poorly executed. The situation reminds me of the early days of e-commerce when the first generation of websites and technologies in the late 1990s were driving the hysteria of the Internet bubble.

The tsunami of opportunity and threat that IoT creates has been written about and forecasted from most every angle.

- There will be nearly twenty billion devices on the Internet of Things by 2020, by which time product and service suppliers will generate revenue in excess of $300 billion.[1]
- Between $4 and $11 trillion per year will be saved through newly found efficiencies by 2025.[2]
- There will be a "redefinition of industry boundaries as the basis for competition, shifting from discrete products to product systems."[3]

The evidence is clear—IoT is going to be a game-changing technology and business strategy.

I spent four years launching and then running Amazon's Marketplace business, the company's monumentally successful platform-play for third-party retailers. I also ran the Amazon Enterprise Services business. Those experiences taught me that it's not the scale of an opportunity that's important but how you approach it.

Since my last book, *The Amazon Way: 14 Leadership Principles behind the World's Most Disruptive Company*, was published in 2014, I have had the opportunity to talk to hundreds of leaders and teams about innovation and the things that get in its way. I've learned about how great companies create systemic change and improvements and about their frustrations as they drive toward innovation and growth.

I've spoken with companies in many industries of every business model and of different sizes, ownership structures, and missions—from insurance companies to utilities to technology-infrastructure companies to nonprofits—and they all look to companies like Amazon in both admiration and fear.

With this book, I started out to create a specific roadmap—a description of how companies and their leaders should approach this transformative opportunity. But the more I thought about it, the more prescribing a specific approach seemed like fool's gold. Even if the approach is a good one and followed to a T, it's unlikely that any company would have the intended results.

Why? Because *methods* are situational. In the companies I've spoken with, there are few golden rules, but there are powerful leadership dynamics that underlie each organization's methods. Those dynamics have had an oversized influence on these companies' successes—or lack thereof.

The leadership philosophies that underlie these companies, however, are much more applicable. They will last over time. And most importantly, there is a clear, winning approach across companies—a common set of principles that are more likely to lead a company to success than failure.

Principles have a vision. Principles adapt to more situations and offer simplifying clarity. Principles can inspire. *Principles are durable.*

CONNECT THE DOTS

In 2005, Steve Jobs gave a commencement speech at Stanford. In life, he said, one's career and interests are varied and random; they would be impossible to coherently plan in advance. Studied in hindsight, however, there are subtle connections between our seemingly dissimilar interests and experiences that create a career.

"You can't *connect the dots* looking forward; you can only *connect* them looking backwards. So you have to trust that the *dots* will somehow *connect* in your future. You have to trust in something—your gut, destiny, life, karma, whatever."[4]

Looking back over my own career, I can see that my dots have connected three distinct passions: *efficiency*, or creating processes that yield better quality with lower costs; *integration* across disparate processes, data, systems, and ecosystems to create seamless capabilities; and the development of *new business models* and capabilities that delight customers.

Those dots started with my degree in industrial engineering, which at its heart is the discipline of building efficient processes and using data for management decisions. They connected to my fifteen years in the systems integration business, designing, testing, and implementing large projects. They've carried over into the past fifteen years, which I've spent focused on strategy and digital reinvention at Amazon.com and for clients as an advisor at Alvarez & Marsal.

As the Internet of Things emerged and quickly gathered momentum, I read articles and books, listened to interviews, and pondered its trajectory. It didn't take long for me to realize that "connected devices" are just another dot that combines my three career passions: efficiency, integration, and new business models.

This book connects these three passions to help you unlock the power of the Internet of Things. I've given you the keys to the ten most important principles I've learned from my many years of experience with Amazon about succeeding in IoT.

THIS BOOK'S ORGANIZATION

Although not required reading, I would recommend reading my first book, *The Amazon Way*, which is newly revised. It provides useful context about Amazon and the leadership principles that guide Amazon's pursuit of opportunities like IoT.

In this book, we will explore IoT in ten principles. These principles are not to be confused with Amazon's own leadership principles, mentioned above. Instead, in this book, each chapter focuses on one principle that will help you move your business successfully into IoT. Each of the ten principles in this book is an important idea or practice that I've identified through my many years working with Amazon and other companies and watching the practices and ideas that have made them successful in innovation and their Internet of Things strategies.

In principles 1 and 2, we'll explore Amazon's focus on customer obsession and how the Internet of Things has become a key tool for improving Amazon's customer experience. In principles 3 and 4, we'll dive into operational excellence through IoT and talk about how to use IoT to power metrics, equations, and algorithms in your business. In principles 5 and 6, we'll explore how to get started in IoT without betting the barn and how to use your existing products in a platform play. In principles 7 and 8, we'll explore the new business models IoT enables. And in principles 9 and 10, we'll talk about how to build disruptive IoT strategies in your industry.

The plan I've written here is not in itself a solution for any one company or individual. To create real meaning, you'll need to ask yourself how these principles apply in your circumstances. But hopefully I've succeeded in translating Amazon's many IoT-related businesses (and some of its competitors) into a set of principles that can start you on your own journey. I encourage you to let me know how it goes.

Let's start by discussing what IoT is and a couple of simple models to improve our ability to describe and formulate a winning IoT strategy for your organization.

John Rossman
Bellevue, Washington

Introduction: IoT Is Not the Watch on Your Wrist (or the Toaster on Your Counter)

In the earliest days of the Internet of Things, insiders liked to describe IoT as what would happen if your wristwatch and your toaster were connected to the Internet. "What if your bread were toasted when the alarm on your wristwatch told the toaster you were waking up?"

It was an exciting and slightly baffling concept. Would I want my bread toasting when I awake each morning? Fortunately, like the Internet, the Internet of Things has matured and become more sophisticated. Let's begin with how it's currently defined and how it's beginning to redefine businesses, cities, and lives.

From a technical perspective, the Internet of Things, or IoT, is made up of a growing body of sensors around the world, collecting and transmitting data. IoT also refers to the rules and events being applied to that data to make adjustments to systems and organizations.

From a conceptual standpoint, IoT is the ability to create digital awareness of the physical world we live in. It's a digital pulse made up of data that we can aggregate to improve the world around us.

From an industry and social perspective, IoT is the basis for reinvention, much the way the Internet was in the 1990s. Some forecast that IoT will be much more powerful, in ways both good and bad. IoT will collect sensor based data from objects as diverse as the human body and the

New York Waterway, allowing them to be sequenced, monitored, and measured with an unprecedented amount of control.

The potential for such a movement in any one segment will be stunning.

Take healthcare, for example, where connected health-monitoring and emergency-notification systems can help us monitor blood pressure and heart rate in real time. Advanced devices are already capable of monitoring specialized implants like pacemakers or hearing aids. Sensors can be installed in living spaces to monitor the health and general well-being of senior citizens. The sensors could monitor the administration of prescription drugs and assist with therapy to regain lost mobility.

End-to-end health monitoring will be available for prenatal and chronic patients, tracking their health vitals and recurring medication requirements. Doctors will be able to monitor the health of their patients on their smartphones after the patients are discharged from the hospital.

Industrial-management systems at hospitals and health centers will be integrated with a "smart grid," enabling real-time energy optimization and resource allocations. Measurements, automated controls, health and safety management, and other functions will all be provided by a large number of networked sensors.

Internet of Things devices will be integrated into all forms of energy-consuming devices—lifesaving medical devices, switches, power outlets, bulbs, and televisions. Those devices will communicate with utility-supply companies to balance power generation and energy usage.

These are just a few of the ways we can expect the Internet of Things to affect one industry. Imagine the many millions of ways we can expect it to impact everything else.

In cities across the world, it's already changing the way that citizens go about their daily lives. In Santander, Spain, a city of 180,000 inhabitants, more than 10 percent of the population has downloaded a smartphone application that gives them access to services like parking search, environmental monitoring, the digital city agenda, and deals from local merchants. More than ten thousand sensors across the city feed into the digital network.

The Sino-Singapore Guangzhou Knowledge City is working on improving air and water quality and reducing noise pollution. San Jose, California, is increasing transportation efficiency, and western Singapore has developed a smart traffic-management system.

The French company Sigfox is deploying an ultra-narrowband wireless data network in the San Francisco Bay Area. By the end of 2016, it plans to set up four thousand base stations to cover a total of thirty US cities.

New York Waterway in New York City has connected all their vessels and monitors them live, twenty-four seven. This also creates exciting new opportunities for applications in security, energy and fleet management, digital signage, public Wi-Fi, paperless ticketing, and more.

We're talking entire cities running in perfect synchronicity here. Now that's big.

That's why, when people tell me that IoT is the watch—or Fitbit—on your wrist, I just smile. IoT is not about one device collecting and sending simple, siloed data back to an individual user. IoT is about the compounded and networked impacts that connected devices can have on our businesses, our lives, and our society.

THE IOT TECHNOLOGY CHAIN

The key technologies of most IoT solutions include sensors, connectivity, cloud storage and processing, analytics, and machine learning. Each of these technologies is making fast strides in capability, cost, operational suitability, standardization and ease of development and deployment. For example, Amazon Web Services (AWS) dropped the cost of one type of cloud storage by forty seven percent in 2016. Printable, flexible and low cost sensors for a wide range of applications are going from research stage to mass production. Developing machine learning capabilities, while still complex, is seeing tools and development platforms come to market allowing a wider range of technology developers to access these capabilities.

The architectures for large IoT deployments continue to quickly evolve. There are always tradeoffs between speed, durability, costs and operational maintenance for a vast array of items with sensors. We are familiar with the cloud processing and storage capabilities, but bringing data back to the cloud to process might not have the speed requirements needed. Sometimes these are processed at the device itself, but sometimes data and events need to be coordinated between items. So a new level called "fog" is being developed as a technology layer between "things" and the cloud. What you can count on is that cost, capability and operational suitability will continue to be on a steep improvement cycle on all areas of the IoT technology chain. While building and integrating the technology will always be hard, the business model and business change are where the real value and challenges will always rise.

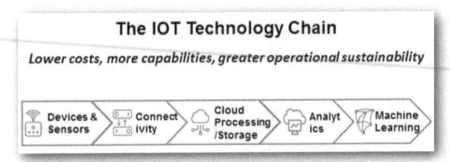

The devices and sensors are not just where the data or event is captured, but often times significant processing occurs there too. Operating systems, software, power supply, the sensors capturing data and events are the key technology components often at the device.

Connectivity is broad set of options for connecting the device to the cloud or to other devices. Many options exist, each with their own considerations. RFID, Bluetooth, wireless, Ethernet (or wired) plus many more are available. The performance, power consumption, cost and operational suitability all vary greatly.

Cloud processing and storage provides the expandable central environment to process and store the data. The geographical nature of the situation, speed and real-time requirements and the volume and variety of data all play a role in the cloud environment.

Typically within the cloud environment is the analytics, event management and data management solutions needed by IoT solutions. This includes the database requirements, event notification and messaging, data visualization and reporting tools.

Machine learning and algorithms are the final component. These are the higher end rules engines and learning algorithms which recognize key optimizations and adjustments to be made in devices. Although often in the cloud, this logic is sometimes in the devices.

Of course this technology chain is not a one-way flow. Alerts, data and adjustments flow back to the devices.

THE IOT TRIPLE THREAT

Basketball coaches often teach their players to get into the triple-threat position—a stance from which they can drive, pass, or shoot the ball. The triple-threat position puts the player in the most advantageous position to make the next best play. It creates the most options for the offensive player, while forcing the defense to prepare for and anticipate all three potential moves.

Similarly, leaders who want to drive the IoT ball down the court need to understand the triple threat of IoT. The IoT triple threat is a framework I've developed by looking at Amazon and other leading companies and their IoT strategies and by working with my clients for over a decade at Alvarez & Marsal.

As we've explored, IoT can help you solve or innovate your way around a vast array of problems. As you build your IoT strategy, though, you can set yourself up for success by leveraging two or more of the IoT triple threats —essentially the three key opportunities created by IoT.

1.   Reinventing the customer experience
2.   Improving operational effectiveness
3.   Developing new business models

Observing Amazon's emerging IoT strategy, it's clear to me that all three of these principles are at the heart of their work, just as they were in the creation of the suite of businesses that now define Amazon as a company, including both the marketplace and enterprise services platforms, which I was responsible for launching.

Reinventing the Customer Experience. Amazon has always been driven to be the most customer centric company in the world. Jeff Bezos's first leadership principle is customer obsession: "Leaders start with the customer and work backwards." It's no surprise that we find this same focus in their approach to the Internet of Things.

Improving Operational Effectiveness. Amazon is also obsessed with operational excellence, constantly improving the customer experience through faster and more accurate order fulfillment. As the company builds out its IoT portfolio, you can expect to see it focus on refining each new vertical it enters to do things faster, with less waste at a lower cost and with higher predictability—all of which lead to operational excellence.

Developing New Business Models. Amazon refuses to be satisfied in any business. It sees itself as a company of inventors and explorers, "thinking big" and refusing to buy into established rules or dogma. Through constant business-model innovation, Amazon has changed the landscape, disrupting business after business—retail, technology infrastructure, logistics, content creation, and distribution. There will be more.

The IoT triple threat is a simple starting point for developing your ideas, strategies, and rationale in IoT, but there is another important angle to understand before we get into principles from Amazon about the Internet of Things.

THE IOT EXTENSIBILITY FRAMEWORK

A FitBit is an example of a connected device, but it is grossly different than a network of sensors tracking and predicting a coordinated set of vehicles. They are both IoT solutions but at two entirely different scales.

To help you understand and classify the different scales and levels of advancement in IoT projects, I've developed a framework to outline important considerations of value, complexity, scale, and impact within a topic or category. For our purposes in gauging IoT solutions, we need a scale that maps capability between really simple IoT cases and robust, complex solutions.

This IoT extensibility framework is not intended to judge a connected device situation or predict the commercial or operational impact it might have in a business. It is most helpful in concept development to build compelling use cases that might start at one place in the framework but have the potential to shift to a different level. In building the business rationale and in architecting a solution, it is helpful to understand how the solution needs to be built today but avoid shortsighted approaches that may eliminate future capabilities. In software design this concept is called "extensibility." The design and implementation take future growth and scenarios into account to make future adaptation easier.

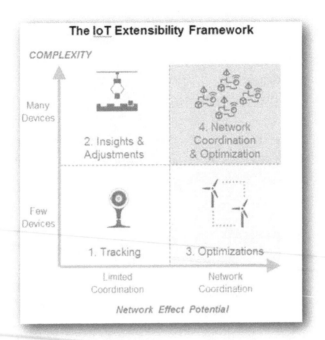

LEVEL 1: TRACKING

Tracking is the basic connected-device scenario. Take, for example, the Google Nest Dropcam. The Dropcam is a motion-activated video camera connected to your home network. You can watch its live feed remotely from your phone or PC—or you can simply set it to record when someone walks by and collect the data in the cloud. The Dropcam is a connected device with sensors. Still, its value is limited. It only provides value to the owner of the data it collects and it is not architected to easily connect with other sources of data.

LEVEL 2: INSIGHTS AND ADJUSTMENTS

Level 2 IoT solutions provide sensor-based analytics that allow thresholds, rules, tracking, and adjustments to be made on basic events and scenarios. Data is captured in the cloud, and minimum algorithms or machine learning are applied. There is no "network" value applied to having many devices connected.

Consumer examples of this stage include many of the current heart rate and running or biking monitors on the market. These capture multiple data points, sync the data to a consumer portal, and allow a user to review the data in various ways.

Many of the traditional industrial manufacturing and logistics sensor applications would also fit into level 2. These systems generally capture production data, feed it into various production and yield reports, and often monitor that data and apply rules. The data or events captured through the system are not systematically combined with other network data and do not create real-time adjustments or optimizations.

These level-2 scenarios tend to be great starting places for an organization. That's because the complete data-management infrastructure for more complete solutions can be put in place at level 2, without having to deal with the hassle of sophisticated math, event management, or adjustments.

LEVEL 3: OPTIMIZATIONS

A single or many of the same devices are connected, and optimizations to performance are made using the data, events, rules, and algorithms across the fleet of devices. This is where "actuators" might be engaged, which are adjusted due to these insights. Optimizations can be based off a single object, perhaps with multiple sensors or one that's coordinating across the network of items.

Examples include a turbine that is adjusted real time based on the flow it is experiencing or a tractor that adjusts fertilizer spread based on the contour and composition of the field. Level 3 optimizations are where complex data science, forecasting, and real-time adjustment scenarios are often found.

LEVEL 4: NETWORK COORDINATION AND OPTIMIZATION

Network coordination provides all the other values we've talked about in levels 1 through 3, with one addition. The insights and actions taken are improved because there are multiple devices and a variety of devices in the network, and the accuracy and insights increase as more devices and the variety of devices are added to the network. Level-4 scenarios provide new partnership and ecosystem strategies and needs.

A trucking company might optimize its fleet based on traffic dynamics or truck telemetry. Firefighting teams might coordinate their efforts based on sensor data from the structure, from firefighting equipment, and from sensors on emergency responders.

The technology and architecture of IoT is complex. They are hard to implement and operationalize. But most of the challenges you'll face in IoT will lie in building the organizational capabilities, culture, and leadership that take advantage of these opportunities.

There is nothing wrong with starting by creating level-1-type tracking capabilities. In fact, depending on your company and goals, I might recommend it. Starting with level-1 capabilities will provide value from the get-go and give you the chance to start building your organizational capabilities and leadership capabilities around using IoT in the business. Down the line, this can lead to better integration with your company and more sophisticated capabilities.

It is most helpful as you develop your concept to help you build compelling use cases, which might have the potential to mature and shift from one level of the maturity curve to another. Use the IoT extensibility framework to understand your situational needs today and avoid shortsighted approaches that would eliminate your ability to move into more-complex capabilities in the future.

Now that you understand the IoT triple threat and can navigate the IoT extensibility framework with the best of them, there's one other major factor you'll need to take into account to give your IoT strategy the best chance at success.

THE POWER OF SWAY

As a partner at the professional-services firm of Alvarez & Marsal, my professional career has been about projects. I've spent the last decade strategizing, architecting, and building digital platforms and capabilities for clients at world-class companies.

Each of these endeavors, and I've been a part of more than a hundred, is structured as a project. Projects are different from operations in two ways: (1) they have a beginning and an end, and (2) they create change. One of my mentors at Alvarez & Marsal is fond of saying that we are not in the status quo–preservation business.

Regrettably, many of the projects I've been a part of launching did not reach the promise or potential they could have reached. In hindsight, were those failed projects due to poor execution? Poor technology or technology strategy? Poor communication?

While all of these are factors that can cause major issues, none is the most common reason that a project fails to reach its potential. Most often, it is the lack of a clear and compelling vision that does a project in. That vision must be defined enough to draw all of the other elements of the project together. And it must come from someone with enough sway within the company to maintain a focus on value.

Without a purposeful and adequate senior leader (CEO, board member, divisional EVP) actively and consistently creating support, providing clearance, and fast-tracking decisions in your IoT strategy, the laws of physics will take hold: a body at rest will remain at rest unless an outside force acts on it.

Many of the principles I've included here are expressly designed to help leaders create and articulate a clear vision for their IoT strategies. By reading this book and following my advice, you'll find it much easier to fill the leadership communication void that so often acts as a black hole for change.

DAY 1 FOR THE INTERNET OF THINGS

Jeff Bezos has long stated that it is still "Day 1" in terms of the impact the Internet will have in society. Amazon, he believes, is in its early days of the business lifecycle. This is such an important leadership message at Amazon that there are two office buildings, Day 1 North and Day 1 South, named after it. Each has a placard with a quote from Bezos tucked inside its entryway.

You might debate about whether that's still true for the Internet itself. In terms of the Internet of Things and the impact it will have in our lives,

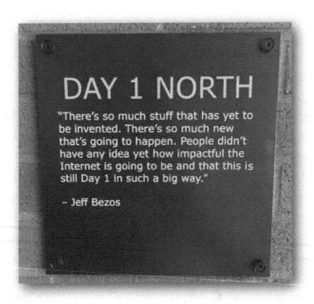

it is definitely still Day 1. Amazon will continue to experiment and invest in customer-facing devices like the Dash Button and Echo as a means of driving the real business opportunity it sees—its Amazon Web Services (AWS) infrastructure and IoT solutions.

Chances are good that you and your company aren't quite so far along in your IoT strategy, but even Amazon feels that it is just starting. Building your strategy and flywheel and having a long-term vision while being impatient and pushing for daily results are all part of the equation.

The "Day 1" mentality also encourages leaders to have a beginner's mind-set and to be open to and curious and humble about new practices and ideas. The expert mind is often closed to seeing new opportunities and innovating beyond the current state.

Principle 1

Reinvent Customer Experiences with Connected Devices

Start with the customer and work backwards.

—Jeff Bezos

"I've fallen, and I can't get up!" Any late-night-TV-watching baby boomer knows the reference to Life Alert, the wearable device that allows the elderly to request medical assistance just by pushing a button.

Life Alert wasn't originally part of the Internet of Things, but it is a button-driven, connected, special-purpose device with many similarities to the IoT products that Amazon and others have launched in the last few years.

Most importantly, Life Alert is a living example of Amazon's first leadership principle—customer obsession. A necklace fob might seem simple, but it fundamentally reinvents the customer experience—both for the elderly, who gain significant autonomy, and for their family members and caretakers, who can feel confident that their loved ones will be able to call for help in case of a fall or other medical emergency.

Customer obsession is a key driver of Amazon's success. The Internet of Things has made it possible for Amazon to gather key insights about its customers' needs and put them to use in real time.

Principle 1: The Internet of Things won't get you anywhere unless you're obsessing over your customers and their experiences and how connected devices can solve their problems.

In this principle, we'll explore the power of customer obsession and how to use the Internet of Things to better understand and serve your customers.

Amazon's Dash, Dash Buttons, and the always-listening Echo are all experiments in special-purpose IoT devices that fundamentally reinvent customer experience. All three enable Amazon customers to order products, get information, and stay connected on the fly.

CUSTOMER OBSESSION

It's no accident that customer obsession is the first of Amazon's official leadership principles. Leaders start with the customer and work backward. They work vigorously to earn and keep customer trust. Although leaders pay attention to competitors, they obsess over customers.

There are two specific concepts to take note of here. First, customer trust—not profit—is the most critical asset Amazon expects its leaders to build. And second, leaders must obsess over customers.

There are plenty of companies and teams out there who claim to be "customer focused" or "customer centered." You may be one of them. But if you don't understand the difference between customer focus and customer obsession, it's unlikely your team will tap into the customer uptake and loyalty that have driven Amazon's incredible growth.

To Amazon, "obsess" means being willing to do really hard things just to make life easier for its customers, frequently in ways that won't drive short-term profit. Often this means literally making the impossible possible.

"Obsession" has meant trying new things, many of which don't work out. It means sticking with the things that do work or that might work instead of getting distracted by the lure of a shinier, more-profitable short-term opportunity.

Most of all, "obsession" means not being stuck in the past. The fact that a product or experience is currently considered "good enough" does not mean that it's good enough going forward. The fact that no one else has put in the effort to create something better is an opportunity, not an excuse to sit back on your laurels. In this never-ending crusade to improve the customer experience, Amazon has innovated, invented, and scaled a long list of historic firsts.

Customer Reviews. When it first launched, Amazon's customer-review feature was controversial, particularly among vendors and brands, who only wanted shoppers to see the positive reviews of their products. (You have to remember that, until this point, brand-controlled testimonials were the main way customers could share their experience with a product.) But Jeff and Amazon were sure of themselves: it might cost a few customers in the short term, they argued, but including negative reviews alongside the positive was the only way to build long-term customer trust. Jeff was right—the move created an important level of customer trust that increased purchasing and loyalty.

Free Everyday Shipping. In 2000, Amazon began offering free shipping for all orders over $100. The catalog world had been the standard bearer for delivery by mail, and their deliveries consistently took ten to fourteen days and cost $6–$10. By 2002, Amazon dropped the purchase threshold to $25. Customers weren't expecting free shipping—it was a new, better level of customer service that didn't seem to have any immediate benefit for Amazon. In fact, the program was called out by analysts, competitors, and the press as unsustainable and irresponsible: Amazon. bomb, they joked. It turned out to be the opposite. For years, the program was Amazon's only marketing effort.

1-Click Ordering. Entering login, billing, and shipping information every time you buy something online is repetitive and time consuming. Doing it once might not be a big deal, but by the time you've done it fifty to a hundred times, you're talking about five hundred plus minutes of your life you won't be getting back. By rolling out 1-Click Ordering in 1997, Amazon allowed customers to skip the shopping cart and confirmation experience for the first time in online-shopping history. In 1999, the company patented that advantage.

Look Inside the Book. When Amazon first proposed it's Look Inside the Book feature, which would allow shoppers to read the first few pages of a book before buying it, publishers and authors were almost universally against it. If customers could tell whether or not they would like a book before buying it, they argued, sales would go down.

But Jeff was bullish: if the book isn't the right fit for the customer, he argued, they should find out *before* they buy it. In the end, Jeff's obsession with building long-term customer trust won out, and Look Inside the Book was launched in 2001, lifting book sales between 5 and 15 percent.

Prime. In 2005, Amazon launched its Prime loyalty program, offering free two-day shipping to members for an annual fee. But the free—and fast—shipping was just the beginning. By building up the appeal of a Prime membership, adding free music, movies, and other benefits, Amazon created a massive moat around its customers.

The free music, videos, and shipping lured Prime members in, but once they had access to all that free shipping, their shopping habits also increased. No need to make extra trips to the store for things like light bulbs and paper towels when you could have them delivered to your door for free in just two days.

Not only had Amazon increased its value per customer—estimates are that a Prime customer spends $1,110 a year, while non-Prime customers spend just $600[5]—but the benefits allowed Amazon to increase its prices. With so many additional benefits delivered to Prime members, Amazon no longer had to be the everyday low-price guy. Its fast, precise delivery had become more valuable.

Autorip. As music migrated online, customers were faced with a dilemma: if they wanted all of their music in one place, they would need to upload every album they'd ever bought on CD, many of which they might have lost or misplaced, to their digital libraries. Amazon couldn't fix this problem, but it could provide its customers with a surprise bonus, something they didn't expect.

That bonus was Autorip—a service that provided Amazon customers with free digital versions of any album they'd ever purchased through Amazon. It was just another of Amazon's moves to build long-term goodwill among its customers rather than focusing on the short-term profits that could have been.

Each innovation on this list was controversial or negatively perceived by industry traditionalists when launched. Naysayers didn't understand Amazon's long-term strategy: obsess over a better customer experience to build long-term trust. But because of that strategy, one-click shopping, free shipping, customer reviews, and countless other Amazon innovations are now the standards by which customers measure all online-shopping experiences.

And, also because of that strategy, we've also seen Amazon confidently lead the way into the IoT product space.

Kindle. The Kindle wasn't the first e-book on the market—Sony launched the Reader in 2006—but it was the first "connected device" pioneered by Amazon. And, like Amazon's entry into online shopping, when Amazon turned its attention to revolutionizing the connected-reading experience, incredible things began to happen. Things that not too long before might have seemed impossible became possible.

Kindle's Whispernet feature let users download books wirelessly to their devices. The Popular Highlights feature suddenly showed users which passages other Amazon readers had already highlighted. By syncing their reading experience across devices, readers could leave their Kindle behind on their nightstand and pick up where they'd left off on their phone or tablet. And Kindle's lending club quickly identified and addressed an early e-book dilemma—how to share a digital library with your friends and family.

To casual observers, the effort Amazon put into creating these features might have seemed foolish—a waste of time and money. After all, Amazon sells both the Kindle Paperwhite and Kindle FireHD *at below cost*.[6] But by keeping the Kindle price low and obsessing over readers' needs, Amazon was building an army of voracious readers, game players, and content consumers. This army was buying more and more of their books and other products through the Kindle platform.

Amazon wasn't making much money on the Kindle, but they were minting money on the products they sold from the Kindle.

Dash and Dash Buttons. A customer-focused Amazon might have been content to sit back and enjoy the spoils of its e-commerce successes, having already revolutionized online shopping. But a customer-obsessed Amazon soon realized that it was missing sales opportunities long before its customers even made it to the website—particularly when it came to household groceries.

Let's think for a minute about restocking household supplies. It sounds boring, but that's exactly how Amazon's Dash program got its start. Let's say you're running low on disposable diapers—a product you really don't want to be caught without. Sometimes you remember to add them to your shopping list, and you pick them up at the store later that day.

But more often you meant to add them to the list but instead got distracted by the dog, which just threw up on the floor, or the ping of a work e-mail. Maybe you accidentally run out of diapers and find yourself in the unenviable position of having to make a late-night run to the store. You drive all the way there, find a parking space, and spend several minutes walking up and down the aisles looking for the diaper section.

When you finally reach the diaper section, you spend a few minutes racking your brain: What size and brand of diapers were you supposed to buy? Is little Betsy still considered a newborn, or is she now a size two? And was it the Pampers or the Luvs that gave her the diaper rash last time? So you buy both sizes just to be safe. Maybe you even buy a few different brands to make sure you won't need to make a return trip.

Somewhere at Amazon, a customer-obsessed team was thinking through this scenario—or perhaps it was one involving garbage bags—when they hit upon the idea for the Dash.

The original Dash was a physical wand, about the size of a Wii controller, that used Wi-Fi to help you order food and pantry items through

Amazon Fresh. All you had to do was scan the item or say its name into the Dash, and it would automatically be added to your Fresh shopping list.

Of course, the wand itself was just part of the overall solution. The wand was connected to cloud infrastructure that stores and processes data—everything from information about the users and how they use the wand right down to the physical items ordered using the wand. From there, machine learning worked to improve the effectiveness of the customer experience, helping to improve photo recognition of items.

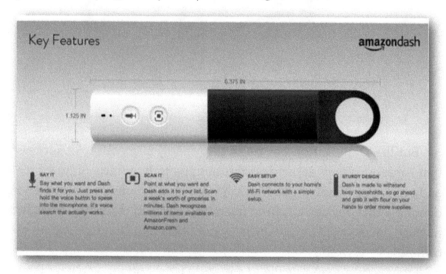

The wand itself never made it out of beta. Instead, its proudest accomplishment became the simpler, more direct Dash Button it spawned. Each Dash Button is a small connected device with an adhesive back: simply stick it next to the Pampers in your baby's room, and push the button when you're running low. Voilà! Your diapers are automatically ordered and shipped.

The button, which was launched the day before April Fools' Day, 2015, was mistaken for a joke by many. Others skipped straight to mockery. "The idea of shopping buttons placed just within our reach," wrote

Ian Crouch for the *New Yorker*, "conjures an uneasy image of our homes as giant Skinner boxes, and of us as rats pressing pleasure levers until we pass out from exhaustion."

But the Dash Button has been surprisingly successful. So successful that Amazon is now expanding the buttons to hundreds of new brands and products. The next generation of Dash is a set of sensors embedded directly within devices like Brita filters and washing machines. No button pushing necessary. They'll reorder water filters and laundry soap on their own.

From widespread ridicule to widespread adoption...you'll remember this pattern from Amazon's most successful e-commerce innovations. Even the business model is familiar: Each Dash Button is $4.99, but you make that money back with an equivalent discount on your first order.

Drones. Amazon's drone delivery program is simultaneously its most magical and it's most predictable IoT innovation to date. I say predictable because, unlike the Dash or the Kindle, drone delivery is not meeting customers in a new place or creating a new purchasing platform. It is simply doing what Amazon has been focused on for a long time—making item delivery faster and faster.

And yet, as building the impossible goes, drone delivery is right up there. Amazon is inventing and building tiny private helicopters to deliver your packages. At the same time, it is fighting extended regulatory and PR battles that have pushed FAA policies to new levels of innovation and fundamentally shifted the public's perception of drones.

Again, to competitors and stock analysts, this might seem crazy. And by the measure of quarterly earnings growth alone—the primary guide-post for most publicly traded companies—it is. Luckily, Jeff thinks about things differently. He and the rest of the Amazon team understand that Amazon's true value proposition is to its customers. In one meeting I was a part of, Jeff told an enterprise client that he couldn't imagine a world where a customer wants a higher price, a slower delivery, or a smaller selection. These were durable customer needs.

By keeping a laser focus on those three durable values and refusing to accept the status quo, Jeff and the Amazon team have made home delivery by drones not only possible but a damn good bet.

That is how innovation and disruption begin—*create better customer experiences.*

PUTTING IOT TO WORK FOR YOUR CUSTOMERS

"This all sounds nice," you might be thinking, "but I'm not Jeff Bezos, my customers need very different things, and we have to generate a profit along the way."

In some ways, you'd be right—nailing the next Kindle or Dash Button for your industry won't be easy. But that's exactly why IoT has become a game changer for those willing to obsess over their customers. The tech-nology and solution components are accessible to every team, the cost basis is much improved and continuing to drop, and you can try small experiments without betting the farm. The key technologies of most IoT solutions include sensors, connectivity, cloud storage and processing, analytics, and machine learning.

Finding even one big success will require lots of experimentation. Many of those experiments will likely fail—just look at Amazon's Fire

Phone or its investment in Pets.com, one of the biggest jokes of the dot-com era. There are nearly unlimited opportunities to improve the customer experience by leveraging connected devices. What's the path?

Start with the Customer. Walk yourself through an entire day in the life of your customer—just as we did earlier with the late-night diaper run. How might connected devices change the way that your product or service fits into that day?

Deep customer obsession is rooted in a company's culture. One way to start building that is through a "voice of the customer" program. One thing to keep in mind about programs like this: successful customer feedback loops aren't relegated to any one product or channel. They span the enterprise and include a deliberate, ongoing mechanism for taking in data from and about your customers. (One survey is not enough.) The good news is that, in a world of connected devices, this is getting easier all the time.

The toughest—and most important—part of the program will be empowering it to create change across the organization. This will require buy-in and collaboration across departments.

Remove Friction. Your next move is to identify and remove points of friction. What problems do your customers face? Why do customers contact you? What parts of your product or customer-service apparatus get in the way of solving those problems? And how could a connected device remove those pain points? Is there data you could be collecting that would give you or your customer new insight?

Sometimes the best way to create a great customer experience is to start by imagining a terrible customer experience. Imagine your grandmother trying to use a cell phone for the first time. No matter how intuitive the process, chances are good that something will go wrong. When it does, she'll spend forty-five minutes on the phone with the nice customer-service agent explaining that "the angry blinkie thingies keep looking at me." If that fails, she'll be forced to drive all the way to her service provider's physical location or, more likely, she'll put the phone away in a drawer until her teenage grandchildren come to visit.

How could you reinvent this experience for her?

Unsurprisingly, Amazon has already tried its hand at this—the Kindle Fire's Mayday feature lets customer service agents take over a user's screen remotely, with their permission, to see and fix problems for them.

As you think about how to reduce friction in your industry, start by recreating a terrible customer experience, and then think about how the Internet of Things or connected devices could improve that experience.

Think Broadly. The next most innovative move in your industry may not directly involve your current product—just think about Amazon's drones. Amazon is an e-commerce company, but it turned out that the design of online-shopping sites and the products they offer are no longer the biggest pain points for customers. The speed and efficiency of their delivery are.

Lastly, across all of these experiences, think about the power of the Internet of Things to provide a new interface to your customers. Connected devices empower you to learn more about your customers and to build deeper insights into your products and services and the environment in which they are used.

What data would help you understand your customers and their experience better? How can you collect that data? And, most importantly, how can you use that data, once collected, to create value and improve your customer experience?

Integrating this kind of thinking into your current customer planning is the key to transitioning from customer focused to customer obsessed.

Principle 2

Enabling Customers
Anytime, Any Way

" **W**ho starred in *Happy Days?*"
"What is the traffic across the 520 bridge?"
"Where is my phone?"
"Turn off the kitchen lights."
"Order more laundry detergent."
"Please get me an Uber to go to the airport."

Humans are inquisitive by nature. We also like to delegate and give out orders. Luckily, responding to questions and orders is what computers do best.

Amazon and its competitors—Google, IBM, Microsoft, and Apple—are investing heavily in personal digital assistants to carry out your every request and answer every question.

Amazon's entrée into that world came in the form of the Echo, a voice-activated speaker system that perches on your kitchen counter. Once connected to your home Wi-Fi and your Amazon account, the personal-assistant software inside of the Echo, called Alexa, can stream music on Amazon Prime, Spotify, and Pandora. Alexa can play your favorite radio stations, turn smart lights on and off, keep track of the whereabouts and status of your car, add to your to-do list, and even order you a Domino's pizza.

But the real significance and future implications of Alexa go far beyond calling you an easy Uber ride.

Principle 2: Customers expect seamless experiences across platforms and channels. The Internet of Things will be instrumental to helping you create this, enabling new interactions that bring ease and delight to your customers.

In this principle, we'll explore how Amazon is using the Internet of Things to build its omnichannel marketing strategy and how you can use Amazon's examples to create a seamless omnichannel strategy for your own business using the Internet of Things.

We'll be talking about Alexa and Echo many times throughout this book because of the many lessons both products have to offer as a multifaceted strategy that creates many opportunities for Amazon. Echo is the physical speaker device, and Alexa is the voice-recognition software that powers the Echo and many other devices. For now, let's start with just one of those—omnichannel.

For Amazon, Alexa is a key part of its omnichannel customer-experience strategy. An existing approach to customer experience, "omnichannel" is the idea that customers' experiences with a company should be seamless across whatever platform or device they might be using.

IoT takes that to the next level, creating new ways to facilitate seamless and interconnected user experiences and gathering data about your customers that helps you to understand and predict their behavior. Omnichannel might sound like a buzzword, but behind that buzzword is a key opportunity that you'll need to understand to get customer experience and IoT right.

More than just a personal assistant, Amazon's Alexa is the first of a new type of computing interface—always on, always listening, and voice activated. Alexa's voice interface creates, facilitates, and encourages new types of customer behaviors that wouldn't be possible with mobile or desktop.

Alexa is the first crack at what could be a meaningful shift in the computing industry from application or browser-based inquiry to a voice-presence-managed interface between people and their world and needs.

It is also the perfect illustration of Amazon's commitment to perfecting omnichannel experiences—the second key to its success in improving customer experience by leveraging IoT.

OMNICHANNEL EXPERIENCE

Retail has likely been impacted by e-commerce perhaps more than any other industry. E-commerce accounts for approximately 10 percent of all retail today and is growing at 20 percent a year. And Amazon is the big winner. Fifty-one percent of all US e-commerce revenue flows through Amazon.

At the same time, customers are expecting more than ever from brands. They want instantaneous service—with a smile. They expect brands to respond not just quickly but twenty-four seven. If you manage to make your customers feel great or inspire a laugh while you're at it, all the better.

This stunning transformation of the traditional retailer market has created a new essential core competency for marketers everywhere: representing and managing your brand and products effectively through multiple channels.

Retailers of just a few years ago were primarily concerned with in-store and catalog sales. Today, the prevalence—and variety—of connected devices means a brand experience must be consistent across Facebook, Twitter, Instagram, Pinterest, any private apps a company has developed in addition to a company's physical location, website, any catalogs it might distribute, and its customer-service lines.

It's not just messaging, language, and imaging. Companies like Amazon, leading the way in marketing, understand that today's customers expect to shop, compare, and purchase across all of those platforms. If they have a question—or a bad experience—they're just as likely to broadcast it across Twitter as they are to call up your customer-service line. If they're shopping for a new product or device, they might start by researching it online and then visit a store to check it out in person.

All of this should be personalized to reflect a customer's browsing, shopping, and customer-service history. Customer *obsession*.

This kind of omnipresent and integrated presence and customer service is the epitome of omnichannel. The omnichannel experience and the opportunity to enable it via IoT is an opportunity in most industries—if you have a customer or provide a product or service, your customers and competitors are thinking about an integrated and improved seamless experience.

MOVING OMNICHANNEL FROM GOOD TO GREAT

The biggest barrier between great omnichannel customer care and mediocre omnichannel customer care is a company's ability to master information continuity. If a customer receives a faulty toaster and lodges a complaint via Twitter or e-mail, that customer's information should be available across all channels. In other words, the manager of that Twitter account should be able to see the e-mail you sent rather than customers having to reexplain the situation.

Luckily, connected devices have risen up to make this kind of customer continuity not only possible but increasingly within reach—even for companies without massive spending or investment capabilities.

For Amazon, it started off simply enough: the company was one of the first to leverage the mobile web by encouraging customers to take photos of products (or their QR codes) they found in the wild and compare them to Amazon's offerings. That information connected to customers' Amazon accounts, which they typically accessed via desktop.

For customers, it's a savings move—they get to see whether there's a better price for the item on the Amazon store. For Amazon, it's a data lead-generation opportunity—they suddenly have access to information about products or services their customers are already interested in buying.

From there, the company evolved into an ecosystem of apps that made online-offline shopping and other Amazon services nearly seamless.

How might you apply the information continuity IoT enables to your business? Let's say you're selling vacuum cleaners. You could skip the whole Internet of Things trend, sell your customers a standard, electric vacuum cleaner, and cross your fingers they don't have any problems or questions.

Or you could sell a connected vacuum cleaner that connects directly to your customer-service agents so that when your customers inevitably call with questions or repairs, you can already see where the vacuum cleaner is and what's wrong with it—"When was the last time you emptied your bags, ma'am? It looks like they're beyond capacity." Or, better yet, you can reach out to them to let them know that their bag is 75 percent full and ask if they'd like to order another.

No bringing the vacuum into a store, no mailing it in for repairs and suffering through dirty floors while you wait. That's superior omnichannel service. And it's only possible when you take advantage of IoT.

In other cases, the most useful data you can collect using connected devices isn't about the product itself. It's about your customers. Where are they? Are they anywhere near a store? What have they searched for lately on your app or website? Can you offer it to them at a discount?

In the last few years, Macy's, GameStop, and a number of other supermarkets and mall developers have been testing something called beacon technology—a small beacon that sits inside a store and can activate the store's app on your phone when you enter the store, sending you alerts about discounts and items on your shopping list.[7]

Instead of a store associate pointing out where the general sales rack is, the beacon actively points out in-store sales that are relevant to you. Put simply, it turns a typical manual and traditional interaction and creates a digital, scalable and personalized version, increasing the average purchase of customers in the store.

HOW TO BUILD A CONNECTED EXPERIENCE, NOT JUST CONNECTED DEVICES

It's easy to get distracted by the prospect of creating one-off connected devices, but too often companies that do this forget about the users' real needs, focusing primarily on flashy features and shiny new technology.

The real promise of IoT devices is in the ways they solve problems for your user.

One helpful way of creating these types of innovative user experiences is IFTTT, or If This, Then That, a free online service that links connected devices and apps using smart recipes. Its catalog of connected devices includes the Amazon Echo, Dash, and hundreds of others. Most importantly, though, each of the recipes it creates is an opportunity to solve a problem for the user, many of which might have previously just been put up with or grown numb to.

You can use IFTTT for many things: if I post a picture on Instagram, then add that photo to my Dropbox account. If I listen to a song on Amazon's Echo, then add that song to a Google spreadsheet. If my Echo alarm goes off, then turn my lights on. If I just parked my BMW, send me an e-mail (or an SMS) with the parking location.

IFTTT isn't just useful as a tool, though. It's also the perfect metaphor to use as you think about ways to improve your customers' experience across multiple channels.

Each recipe consists of a trigger—say, sending an e-mail—and the impact that trigger causes—scheduling an automatic follow-up to that e-mail. If "this" happens—you send an e-mail—then "that" should also happen—Gmail should schedule an automatic follow-up.

As you're developing your IoT strategy, connected devices provide an opportunity to identify a trigger, put evaluation and logic around that trigger, and then specify another action or actions to take place. Anything a sensor can measure or detect can be used in this way.

I suggest you take some time to apply this to your business.

What are the If This, Then That scenarios in your customers' experiences?

What events would you like to capture?

Let's assume a customer stops in your store to look at an item. What does that mean? Should you send them an e-mail? A discount on that item? What experience would add value to your brand for them? Next, how can you capture that using a smart device? It's likely that, using IoT, you can create some kind of sensor to capture that event—the moment the customer comes within a certain radius of a certain point—and then create the logic to react to it.

This is a simple exercise and approach you can take to improve customer experiences through IoT. Don't worry about how to enable these at first. Just start with the brainstorm.

Of course, not every IFTTT scenario will be worth pursuing. You should be looking for IFTTT scenarios driven both by a business case and your own intuition.

- Are you going to create a better customer experience and gather valuable data from this experience?
- Is it economically feasible?
- How do you test this in an agile, small manner at first?
- Will it really give you the benefit you expect?

Assuming your ideas pass the sniff test, building your own IFTTT recipes can be the perfect way to put yourself in an IoT mind-set.

THINK BIG

As you develop strategies for IoT-enabled omnichannel marketing and customer service, there's one specific trap you should work to avoid. Don't limit yourself by defining a device as something that can fit in the palm of your hand. In some cases, one of the most important devices people own really only fits inside their garages. Yes, I'm talking about their cars.

Ford, Audi, Tesla, and others have spent years building computers into their cars. "Today's car has the computing power of 20 personal computers, features about 100 million lines of programming code, and processes up to 25 gigabytes of data an hour," a 2014 McKinsey report boasted.[8]

As car companies focus more and more on integrating connectivity into their vehicles, your car is becoming one of the most-powerful connected devices you'll own.

There's a problem with this though—distraction. Most computing interfaces are built on touch—swiping, hitting buttons, typing—all of which can be extremely distracting to drivers. If only there were a hands-free interface that would let drivers interact with their connected cars while keeping their hands on the wheel and their passengers safe...oh, wait.

You can see why Amazon is partnering up with Ford's SYNC infotainment system to integrate the SYNC infotainment system with an Alexa-powered Echo speaker. Ford, which has been a pioneer in the connected car field, expects to have forty-three million SYNC-enabled vehicles on the road by 2020.

Yes, the Echo device is spreading through homes across America, helping people turn on and off their lights, create their shopping lists, and order new groceries. But it's not just at home that you might want to take advantage of Alexa. How many times have you been driving when you were hit with sudden doubt—did I turn off the oven? What about the kitchen lights? Did I lock the door? Remember to arm the security system?

Alexa, integrated into your Ford SYNC system, can do all of those things for you.

That's a physical omnichannel experience that blows social media integration out of the water.

And Alexa isn't Amazon's only omnichannel IoT play. By focusing on the car as a major part of its omnichannel equation, Amazon is also working on one of its key customer obsessions from principle 1: faster, more convenient delivery.

Let's say you order something from Amazon. You're a busy person, so chances are you won't be home to sign for it when it arrives. But you're sick of package theft from your porch, and you don't have time to pick it up from the office of the delivery service itself, which is often all the way across town.

A new test partnership between Amazon, Audi, and DHL is allowing some Audi owners to skip the delivery-planning hassle altogether.

Instead, they're delivering customers' packages straight to the trunks of their cars.

How does it work? On the day of delivery, you consent to location tracking during a set time window—far preferable to relegating yourself to the house for that window. During that time, a DHL truck will find your car and pop the trunk using a single-use digital access code. As soon as the trunk closes again, the code expires, and the trunk locks, leaving your package safe and sound inside your locked car.

Amazon's partnerships with Ford and Audi are still early and experimental. In the end, they may not prove to be killer use cases. But they do begin to set an example for how companies can facilitate user experiences across channels—particularly across traditionally nonintegrated channels—using IoT.

As customers' expectations about where and when they should be able to connect with brands grow, the Internet of Things will become an integral enabler. It will allow companies to create seamless and connected experiences with their products and services—not just across all channels but longitudinally, across the entire life cycle of their products, and the experiences of their customers.

Principle 3

Relentless.com—Continuous Improvements via Connected Devices

One of the more unique aspects of working at Amazon is that every-thing—every process, every customer experience, and every func-tion—has an improvement plan and roadmap. Compare that with the typical company, where, other than the occasional reorganization, pro-cesses that aren't broken stay largely the same from year to year.

You can find nods to this focus on continuous improvement all throughout Amazon's leadership principles and history. Bezos originally named his company Relentless.com. In fact, if you type "www.relentless. com" into a browser, it will still take you to Amazon.com. While he ulti-mately decided against such a literal moniker, "relentless" still perfectly encompasses Amazon's nature. The company is dead set on constantly exploring and reinventing itself through key leadership principles and an undying belief in the power of technology.

For Amazon, IoT is the latest big opportunity to stay relentless.

Principle 3: Connected devices are a powerful enabler for monitor-ing and improving your operations to make your company more effi-cient, competitive, and profitable.

In this chapter, we'll explore the tools Amazon and others use to think about ways that connected devices can reengineer a company's current processes and capabilities to improve quality, decrease waste, reduce cycle times, and, as a result, decrease costs.

Amazon's dedication to continuous improvement is a key part of company culture.

Even the teams and team leaders that aren't sure whether their projects will get funded have a deep understanding and written articulation of how their idea will scale if it does. That focus on how to do more with less means that projects that *are* funded can hit the ground running. Leaders already know how a project will improve the customer experience *and* how it will reinforce Amazon's flywheel. The Amazon flywheel is the strategy Bezos created to explain how customer experience would reinforce its larger business goals and vice versa. (We'll talk more about that in future chapters.)

This company-wide expectation is reinforced by things like Amazon's evaluation process, which assesses employees for, among other things, their commitment to continuous improvement. "Always looks for ways to make Amazon.com better," the standard reads. "Makes decisions for long-term success. Investigates and takes action to meet customers' current and future needs. Not afraid to suggest bold ideas and goals. Demonstrates boldness and courage to try new approaches."

Amazon's approach to process improvement illustrates the fact that there are really two kinds of innovation. "Big I" innovation is what comes to mind for most people when you talk about innovation. It generally leads to a new product or feature or a completely new experience. In the best cases, those experiences feel like magic. (Think about drone delivery or PrimeNow's two-hour delivery program.)

But there's another type of innovation that's just as—if not more— important to a company or product's success. And, as Amazon has demonstrated, it's one of the most consistent ways to take your products, services, and processes from good to great. This kind of innovation is focused on the continuous refinement and improvement needed to create frustration-free customer experiences. I call it "little i" innovation, commonly known as continuous improvement.

Of course, Amazon is just one of many companies that have found value through a focus on continuous improvement. It's likely you're at least familiar with one or more of the business methodologies it has inspired.

- **Lean**—the philosophy of creating more customer value with fewer resources.
- **Toyota Production System**—management approach intent on eliminating all waste, which includes key strategies such as "Just in Time" inventory and demand signals.
- **Statistical Process Control, or SPC**—a system of attaining and maintaining quality through statistical tools that emphasizes root-cause elimination of variation.
- **ISO 9000 Quality Management**—a set of quality certification standards based on eight management principles, including continuous improvement and fact-based decision making.
- **Six Sigma**—a data-driven methodology for eliminating defects, reducing costs, and eliminating waste.

All of these strategies empower employees at the companies that use them to gather data and to act on the insights that data provides. They are encouraged to drive change and improvement from within. But each of these strategies was also created before IoT.

The introduction of ubiquitous connected devices has changed the rules of the data game, creating the possibility for real-time feedback loops that power continuous improvement programs.

Instead of living in a world of manual data collection, which creates limited, slow, and stale data sets, IoT creates an exponential stream of affordable real-time data. That flood of data empowers companies to focus on the continuous improvements to their internal systems, saving them time and money while increasing productivity and consistency.

HOW AMAZON TOOK OPERATIONS FROM GOOD TO GREAT

Today Amazon's operations—the way they fulfill, ship, track, and deliver your orders—are world class. But they didn't start out that way. Amazon measured, refined, and executed its way to greatness. It embraced continuous improvement as a way of life.

By building that dedication into its company culture, creating an operational-improvement heritage, Amazon has been able to build out consistently high-quality, low-cost facilities all around the world. They now boast three hundred fulfillment centers across fourteen countries.[9]

This kind of consistency gives Amazon the confidence and competence to guarantee incredible service: Amazon Fresh, Amazon's home grocery delivery service, lets customers schedule delivery within a fifteen-minute window. That kind of customer service takes incredible forecasting and execution capability—ability built on the back of Amazon's world-class supply-chain heritage.

That level of precision wouldn't be possible if Amazon hadn't made a concerted effort to take advantage of connected devices and the data they provide.

In the early 2000s, the leaders of Amazon's fulfillment and operations capabilities decided to implement Six Sigma, a data-driven five-step approach for eliminating defects in a process. Define, measure, analyze, implement, and control—or as it is referred to in Six Sigma, DMAIC. This is the root improvement cycle in Six Sigma and sets up the methodical, measured steps and mind-set to squeeze out defects, costs, and cycle times.

Six Sigma was introduced by Bill Smith, an engineer at Motorola, in 1986. In 1995, Jack Welch used it at General Electric to much success. The term itself is used to describe a manufacturing process that is defect-free to six standard deviations. In other words, the process is 99.9996 percent accurate.

One of the challenges of completing a Six Sigma initiative is that so much of the effort—generally up to 25 percent—lies in collecting data. Depending on the project, manual data collection can be not only difficult but inaccurate. The data itself is often of questionable quality, skewed by bias or cut short due to time and effort.

Because of these challenges, Six Sigma certifies professionals in a set of empirical and statistical quality-management methods to help them execute on the process successfully. These professionals are installed in an organization during a Six Sigma process to make sure everything is completed successfully.

There are several levels of Six Sigma certification, but the most involved is called a Black Belt. Black Belt practitioners have received significant training and are deeply vested in applying Six Sigma, dedicating 100 percent of their time to its application. It takes a certain kind of person to be a great Black Belt. Black Belts are generally nimble problem solvers, good project managers, and facilitators. They are crafty at collecting data and have a strong background in statistics and math.

As you can imagine, these kinds of people are also highly sought after and well compensated. Creating a team of Black Belts within your organization is one of the biggest cost drivers of Six Sigma initiatives.

That's where IoT comes in.

Using connected devices to collect data frees up the Black Belts in an organization to tackle more projects. It also leads to faster Six Sigma initiatives and a much richer, more reliable data set.

Connected devices can bring visibility to your company's operating conditions, giving you real-time insight into the flow, status, and state of key items in your process. Not only does this enhance your understanding of needed improvements, but it builds a way to scale operations with active quality and measure built into the process.

At the time Amazon integrated Six Sigma into its operations, the company was experiencing a disconnect in a process it calls SLAM. SLAM stands for the ship, label, and manifest process. Every time something, like a printer, is ordered on Amazon, that printer is placed in a box in an Amazon fulfillment facility, labeled, sorted, and shunted through the fulfillment center, until eventually it's placed in an outbound truck. That's the SLAM process. At peak, Amazon ships over one million packages a day.

When Six Sigma was introduced, packages were labeled and moved down conveyor belts before being manually sorted and delivered to the correct docking station. This worked well most of the time, but there was no final confirmation that the package had actually made it onto the right truck, and there was no visibility—for the company or the customer—about where exactly a package was in the outbound process. As a result, packages were occasionally missorted.

An occasional missort doesn't sound like a big deal, but over the course of a year, missorts can cost a company like Amazon millions of dollars. More importantly, even one missort breaks Amazon's underlying promise to its customers: the promise that all of their orders will arrive in their hands on time.

For Amazon, the solution was to create a positive automated confirmation, or "visibility," that a package had moved correctly through all logistics checkpoints after its shipping label had been applied. The change was simple in concept but incredibly complicated in implementation.

To execute, Amazon installed sensors and readers across its conveyor system. The sensors would automatically scan a package's barcode as it moved through the SLAM process. Since packages were scanned to destination-specific staging areas, the sensors allowed Amazon to track the whereabouts of specific packages at any given time in the SLAM process. Furthermore, as Amazon employees loaded those packages into the outbound trucks, scanners on the bay doors would alert them if a package was about to be loaded into the wrong truck.

By creating a positive-confirmation system for its packages, Amazon lowered its missorts to within Six Sigma's 0.0004 percent accuracy range. That's fewer than four packages missorted in every million.

In Amazon's SLAM process, the IoT answer was relatively complicated to implement. In many continuous improvement cases, though, IoT-based solutions can be exceedingly simple.

For example, if you run a corporate facility, in many states you are required by law to schedule monthly inspections of every fire extinguisher in that facility and file a report. It's an incredibly important rule from a safety and liabilities perspective, but it's also an operational challenge to schedule and complete. As a result, companies often miss a month here or there. Enter en-Gauge, a company that sells connected fire extinguishers. en-Gauge's solution alerts a building's security system if an extinguisher becomes noncompliant. It will also notify a facility manager if an extinguisher is pulled from its mount. The savings are not only in manual labor but in the accuracy of the inspection.

INTEGRATING IOT-DRIVEN CONTINUOUS IMPROVEMENT INTO YOUR OPERATIONS

You may be struggling to imagine how connected devices could empower and supercharge process improvements in your company. That's OK. There are several questions that you can ask yourself to help identify situations that might benefit from an IoT-driven continuous improvement process.

1. *What operating condition information would be valuable to your company?* Let's say you operate a truck fleet. One of the largest operating costs and safety issues in trucking is tire wear and maintenance. Tires are expensive and wear out relatively quickly because of the weight of the load they carry and the long distances truckers travel. A punctured tire can lead to lost goods, but it's also the cause of many accidents. Sensors and real-time data about tires could help a driver or a trucking company monitor tire wear, tread, and air pressure to avoid acute tire compromise.

2. *What manual data entry or logging is done in your business today?* Across the health care industry, a huge amount of data is being collected about patients every day. Nurses measure and record patients' temperatures, blood pressures, and medications, among many other things. Using machines that automatically record that data in a patient's file would not only save money but would mean fewer errors made and more lives saved.

3. *What is the incomplete and inaccurate data in my business?* Imagine you run a sales team. You'd like to be sure that that team

is out making a certain number of visits or stops every day, but tracking every sales associate—or even asking them to track themselves—is a tremendous burden. There's also a huge variety in the accuracy and amount of data that different teams may choose to input into a company's CRM system. Where did each salesperson go? How long did that person stay? How many outbound calls did an associate make? All of this could be captured with sensors and devices.

4. *What inspections and audits are done today?* en-Gauge, which we mentioned above, is one example, but any kind of regular inspection or internal audit can be a great candidate for automation. Picture a storage bin full of Kindles in an Amazon fulfillment center. Simply adding a weight sensor to the bin (otherwise known as a scale) would allow the company to consistently reconcile its physical inventory with what's recorded in its inventory system.

5. *What shrinkage, damage, or underutilization occurs in the business?* Hospitals are a great example of a situation where equipment is costly, mobile, and critical. Knowing where critical equipment, like a crash cart, is and whether it's ready for use is mission critical in a hospital. Real-time location systems, or RTLSs, is an entire category of IoT solutions providing information about the whereabouts and operating state of medical equipment.

6. *What are the operating risks?* Knowing—and tracking—key operating risks can save millions of dollars and help you avoid catastrophic risk. The oil and gas industry is aggressively adding sensors into their pipeline systems so that they can have real-time information about operating risks or weaknesses in pipeline systems. PG&E, which operates tens of thousands of miles of pipeline, even taps into data from fire, transportation, and civil emergency-response systems to identify risks.[10]

7. *What are the quality issues and drivers of customer contacts?* Think about what information would provide insights into the root causes of problems with your product that your customers might

experience. What sensor would identify or create an indication of the situation? As a customer, I don't know if I have a furnace or AC issue until it happens or unless I schedule a routine maintenance check-in. A sensor installed in those machines could remind you that it's been six months since you switched your air filter or that there's a 75 percent probability that a part will fail within the next three months.

SPECIAL SNOWFLAKE? THINK AGAIN

I was recently challenged by a potential client who felt that his company was already world class in its operations. There really wasn't much opportunity, he said, for ongoing operational improvement through the Internet of Things. I told him the story of General Electric.

GE is renowned, and often copied, for its operational excellence. The company is widely considered a leader in the adoption of Six Sigma across many aspects of business. In spite of all this, GE sees operational improvement through IoT as a monumental opportunity. In 2015, GE announced that it would be rebranding itself as the "Digital Industrial Company," using IoT to drive improvements not only in its operations but to create new businesses. As CEO Jeff Imelt wrote in his 2015 annual letter, "We accelerated our transformation as a leader in the Industrial Internet, becoming a 'Digital Industrial' company. In the Industrial Internet we see the next great wave of productivity—both for our company and for the customers we serve. We are a company that invests in broad industrial transitions, and they don't come much bigger than the full application of data and analytics to machines and systems."[11]

If GE is betting the business on IoT to drive the next wave of operational improvement, I'm betting that your company can find ways to improve even world-class capabilities.

The trick? You just have to be relentless.

Principle 4

Do the Math—How IoT Enables Better Insights and Analysis

It's often said that you don't really understand something until you can express it as an algorithm. As Richard Feynman said, "What I cannot create, I do not understand."[12]

—PEDRO DOMINGO, *THE MASTER ALGORITHM*

In 2004, I attended a senior executive team meeting at Amazon that just so happened to coincide with the Salesforce.com IPO. During the meeting, one of the other executive team members casually commented that Salesforce was the world's largest customer relationship management (CRM) technology company.

Big mistake.

A senior Amazon leader (guess who) immediately reacted. *"We are the world's largest CRM company!"*

The point was clear. Like a CRM company, Amazon is obsessed with managing and analyzing the data around customer interactions to improve its relationships with them. And it is doing it on a much bigger scale than Salesforce. The digital nature of Amazon's business and its focus on collecting obscene amounts of data actually make it significantly different than the average e-commerce company.

IoT empowers you to collect data about what's going on in your business at a scale and magnitude never seen before. But unless, like Amazon, you're willing to take that data and develop models, analytics, and algorithms and "do the math" around what this data means, you'll miss out on the value of this huge asset.

Principle 4: Using mathematical equations and the Internet of Things, you can track the levers and processes of your business, learn more about specific processes, and gather data that will power and inform those equations, driving improvements and efficiencies.

In this chapter, I'll take you through the basics of how Amazon and other leading companies use analytics and algorithms to improve their business.

AN EXPLOSION OF DATA

Most organizations primarily collect core transactional data used to run their business—orders processed, inventory tracking, customer interactions, and financial transactions. The Internet, of course, has created a new sphere of data collection that's richer than that core transactional set, but the Internet of Things is leading to a data explosion.

It is estimated that the "data universe" is doubling every two years. Ninety percent of all stored data has been generated in the past two years. By 2020 there will be forty zettabytes (forty trillion GBs).[13] The amount of stored data generated by IoT will grow from 2 percent in 2013 to 10 percent by 2020.

One of the biggest risks for a businesses in this environment is that they spend valuable time and resources collecting data, but they aren't actually able to use that data to successfully drive business outcomes.

You may not be surprised to hear that at Amazon, there is a specific and methodological way of tracking and analyzing data to inform business decisions. It's an essential step in taking advantage of the power of Internet of Things, as we've been discussing it so far.

AMAZON'S CULTURE: IN GOD WE TRUST. ALL OTHERS MUST BRING DATA

Amazon.com has a culture of data-driven decision-making and demands insights and recommendations that are timely, accurate, and actionable. At Amazon, you will be working in one of the world's largest and most complex data environments.[14]

—Multiple Amazon job listings

On one Wednesday afternoon, I stepped into the office of an Amazon senior finance leader. There on his wall was a poster bearing Edward Deming's famous quote: "In God We Trust. All Others Must Bring Data."

It was a clear measure of the culture across Amazon, where as much or more time is spent defining and agreeing on how to measure a new feature, service, or product as designing the feature itself. Teams spend weeks considering the inputs and outputs of an operation and what data might be needed to run that operation and understand its complex internal workings.

The general scope of that approach follows four steps:

Step 1. Define the decision-making logic. Develop a strong understanding of how decisions in a process are currently being made and how they should be made.

Step 2. Build an equation (or equations) to describe that decision-making logic.

Step 3. Improve the data you're collecting (use connected devices as part of your approach).

Step 4. Use that data to power the formulas. Use the formulas to drive the decision-making logic.

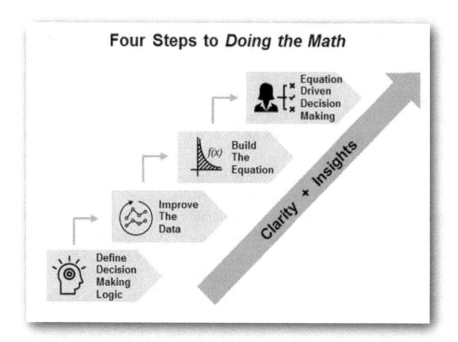

A small subset of teams are focused on bigger, long-term capabilities. They take this focus even further by creating mathematical equations to model key business functions they're responsible for tracking. These equations are known as fitness functions.

In addition to the insight a fitness function provides, its development builds clarity and agreement around the core values and accountability of the team. Unlike standard team metrics, a completed fitness function has to be approved by Amazon's executive team.

We used to joke that getting a fitness function approved was more difficult than getting canonized.

Once a team has agreed on its metrics (or, in some cases, its fitness function), the team's weekly rhythm is defined by a cascading set of metrics meetings. A successful metrics meeting includes clear conversations about what happened during the course of the week and why. The team will identify any needed fixes or adjustments, as well as who will be responsible for the implementation of those fixes. Although these meetings are called "metrics meetings," really what they are is "account-ability" meetings.

The saying "If you can't measure it, you can't manage it," is company religion. To ensure accountability, the ownership of each metric is assigned to an individual. This happens even if, as is often the case, all of the factors driving that metric aren't in the owner's reporting structure. As the owner of a specific metric, you are expected to seek its improvement and understand its root cause factors.

Accountability isn't the only benefit of this approach. The approach also lessens bureaucracy and keeps organizational structure from interfering with progress. A team can operate relatively autonomously once its metrics are approved. It can set its own priorities and identify innovation strategies.

So team metrics keep individual teams in line, but how does Amazon make sure the larger company is progressing on schedule in the right direction?

To keep teams accountable to one another and set high-level standards, Amazon relies on another level of accountability known as a service-level agreement (SLA). SLAs are guarantees of critical performance that can exist not only internally between teams but also externally between Amazon and its customers or other third parties.

An SLA that guarantees on-time order delivery might apply to a range of teams within the company, but it also sets accountability to third-party vendors and customers. On a daily basis, a team's metrics will be vigorously compared to SLAs.

INSTRUMENTATION: REAL-TIME, FINE-GRAINED DATA

Once a team's metrics and SLAs are in place, the focus turns to data collection that will inform those metrics and SLAs. At Amazon, there are very specific standards for the quality and type of data a team should collect. Amazon's executive team refers to those standards as "instrumentation."

Expectations around data collection—or instrumentation—at Amazon are twofold: First, data should be fine grained in nature. You can always summarize and aggregate data, but you can't go back and derive more detail from a dataset.

Secondly, that data should be available in real time. You can always batch data up or slow it down, but you can't always speed it up. Design for no time lags and no batch systems.

There are lots of reasons this is important. Let's say a grocery company uses a refrigerated storage bin to keep its fruits and vegetables fresh. Suddenly, over the course of a day, all the lettuce goes bad. If the company has been collecting fine-grained data—for example, any changes in temperature or pressure and their time stamps—that grocery company might actually be able to figure out what it was that caused the lettuce to go bad. Otherwise, they're stuck wondering about the possible variables and causes in that situation.

Of course, it's not possible to collect fine-grained real-time data in every situation. There are limitations to the nature of the data that you're able to collect in a specific situation, but at Amazon it's expected that you will work vigorously to achieve instrumentation.

SCALING DATA COLLECTION AND WORK

In some cases, it doesn't yet make sense to use connected devices and the Internet of Things to collect data. If you're conducting a trial or a short-term low-tech experiment, you might actually want to collect some data manually. And some mundane or routine tasks actually can't be automated.

In those cases, it's best to sit back and accept that what you're facing is really what Bezos calls OPW, or other people's work. These are tasks that you don't want your team members wasting their time or talent on. In these cases, your goal should be to figure out how to get others to do these mundane, routine jobs. Luckily, Amazon has built a service for exactly this situation. It's called Mechanical Turk.

Amazon Mechanical Turk is a marketplace for work that requires human intelligence. The Mechanical Turk service gives businesses access to a diverse, on-demand, scalable workforce and gives workers a selection of thousands of tasks to complete whenever it's convenient.

Amazon Mechanical Turk is based on the idea that there are still many things that human beings can do much more effectively than computers, such as identifying objects in a photo or video, performing data deduplication, transcribing audio recordings, or researching data details. Traditionally, tasks like this have been accomplished by hiring a large temporary workforce (which is time consuming, expensive, and difficult to scale) or have gone undone.[15]

When developing an OPW strategy, one option is to turn to Mechanical Turk. Still, even with Mechanical Turk, you'll face quality problems. Any time a person is involved, you'll face limits to the data collected, real labor costs, and, in some cases, lag time.

If at all possible, you should automate even basic data collection.

CONVERT ANALOG TO DIGITAL

One of the inherent benefits of a native digital business is the ability to collect much more data than traditional businesses in the course of day-to-day business operations. That extra data is known as "digital exhaust." When a company's core business and customer experiences are digital in nature—centered mainly on desktop, mobile, or some other e-commerce model—it's relatively easy to collect metrics and measures across the business.

While all digital businesses throw off this digital exhaust, only some collect enough of it to create the formulas and algorithms that would improve business outcomes. A company that successfully uses its digital exhaust might combine the browsing and online-shopping history of a customer with buying history of other customers in their segment to make personalized recommendations or offers, either while they are shopping or later over e-mail.

This is in contrast to traditional businesses and processes (think about your average corner grocer or distributor), which don't have that inherent data advantage. Any data captured is typically the result of required transactions or key process steps. And much of it is collected and input manually.

The nature of these analog processes creates high costs and high barriers to collect lots of data and, just as importantly, makes it very difficult to make real-time adjustments.

IoT is the "analog to digital world" converter.

By installing sensors in everyday processes, an analog business can actually put the plumbing in place to create and collect the same insights and instrumentation as a purely digital process.

Obviously, even with IOT, there are real costs of collecting, transmitting, processing, and storing data. Those costs mean that there needs to be thoughtful rationalization about how much data is enough. Still, relative to the data-starvation diet most existing processes rely on today, the opportunities for data collection among even small analog businesses are huge.

THE SKINNY ON ALGORITHMS

The general perception of algorithms is that they're extremely complicated and opaque. And they can be, but don't let this intimidate you. Algorithms are really just formulas or rules that use data to make a prediction, recommendation, or decision. Oftentimes, the best algorithms are fairly simple rule-based systems that help smart humans scale their decision making.

You can use algorithms to make real-time improvements in your business process based on outside or external factors or to make better decisions about the things you need to do.

An algorithm could be used to optimize a warehouse worker's pick path (the route he or she takes through the picking area of a warehouse while selecting merchandise). It might use historical information to recommend how much inventory to purchase. It might even determine which promotion to offer customers based on their purchase history or browsing data.

How do you start? It all starts with being able to define what question or problem you are trying to answer or optimize and then "do the math" to create the formula and define the variables. (More on that in just a second.)

At some point in the process, you will need to employ true mathematical expertise to turn amateur rules and algorithms into robust and sophisticated applied mathematical models. If that sounds expensive, it's because it is. But it's also worth it.

Bezos wrote about this in Amazon's 2010 shareholder letter. After giving readers a glance into the computer and data science advancements they have used to scale their business, he wrote, "Now, if the eyes of some shareowners dutifully reading this letter are by this point glazing over, I will awaken you by pointing out that, in my opinion, these techniques are not idly pursued—they lead directly to free cash flow."[16]

HOW TO GET STARTED IN YOUR BUSINESS? *DO THE MATH*

> *Measurement is the first step that leads to control and eventually to improvement. If you can't measure something, you can't understand it. If you can't understand it, you can't control it. If you can't control it, you can't improve it.*
>
> —H. James Harrington

Do you know the formula for your business process? Do you know what the input variables are versus the output variables? Working with my clients, I do a significant amount of process-reengineering and process-improvement work.

When I get started, an early question (and test) I give is to ask three questions:

1. First, do you have a sufficiently deep and accurate definition of the process?
2. Second, can you walk me through a balanced (cost, quality, throughput) set of metrics for the process (and show me today's metrics in addition to last month's metrics)?
3. Third, can you write me a formula for the process?

The answers tend to range. Many have a definition of their process, but it's not deep or accurate enough to explain how their business really works. Most have some metrics, but they're generally single sided or unbalanced. And as for that last question—a formula for their business process? Most often I work with clients who have no idea what a formula for their business might look like.

What would it look like to really understand these things about your business?

Let's take a deeper look at the case of Clifford Cancelosi, an ex-Amazon leader and former colleague of mine. Until recently, Clifford was a leader at a national home-service appliance-installation and repair business.

When Clifford started in the home-repair business, customers were consistently waiting seven to ten days for a scheduled appointment with a technician. This made it hard to create a business roadmap or even to prioritize the urgency of specific customers.

Luckily, based on his Amazon experience, Clifford knew what to do. He calls it "do the math." So he set to work creating a set of equations to determine his daily effective repair capacity. After some thought, he realized that, at a high level, the company's effective daily repair capacity for each technician was a function of three variables:

- The mean time it takes a technician to complete a job
- The mean time it takes a technician to move from job to job
- The percentage of times a repair job was completed in one visit

The formula for the effective capacity of a technician is then this:

(eight hours * percentage first-time completes) / (mean time to complete job + mean touting time between jobs) = effective daily capacity

So, if the mean time to complete the job is 2 hours, the mean time to move between job locations is 0.5 hours, and the percentage of first-time completes is 75 percent, the effective capacity becomes

(8*.75) / (2+.5) = 2.4

That's 2.4 effective jobs per eight-hour day.

Once Clifford had this equation, he could turn each variable into a metric—first-time completes, mean routing time, and so forth. He tracked each to keep tabs on that specific part of the business's operations.

From there, he analyzed the possible errors that might affect each metric. In the case of first-time completes, these included the following:

- Technician efficacy
- Wrong part on truck
- No part on truck
- Scheduling inaccuracy

The more the company grew to understand the subequations within the formula and what drove variations in each metric, the better understanding they had of how to improve business performance. That deep understanding allowed the company to build formulas to augment its manual decision making.

Today, that home-appliance-repair business has significantly improved its effective capacity formula. It has strengthened its first-time complete metric by creating a hierarchy of metrics that measures the critical customer experience and the root causes of each metric to improve the metric, reduce variability, and reduce costs.

If you're struggling to understand how to measure and improve your business processes, this is a great way to start.

1. Pick a key process or customer experience. (In this case, the number of jobs a technician can complete in a day.)
2. Define the hierarchy of metrics. (What are the factors that affect that process?)
3. Build a formula from the variables.

Once you have your basic formulas, it becomes much easier to understand which parts of the processes could benefit from more data collection by connected devices.

In Clifford's appliance repair business, for example, sensors were used to capture

- *The actual routes of company delivery trucks and the actual time between stops using company-provided tablets.* Once the company had actual route and wait-time data, they overlaid it with a driver's planned route and expected routing time to identify factors that might improve the efficiency of drivers—for example, eliminating unscheduled stops, increasing productivity on each job, and creating more efficient routes for drivers.
- *The movement of key inventory using RFID sensors.* RFID sensors allowed company leaders to see when key inventory was loaded on a truck and when it was removed. This not only helped eliminate shrinkage, but it allowed them to prepare for inventory needs.

The next step for the appliance-repair business would be to work with appliance manufacturers to include connected sensors in the appliances themselves. That would allow the company to understand the problem with the appliance—and any needed parts—before the technician arrives, leading to better "first-time fix" metrics and, eventually, the ability to detect, model, and predict appliance failures.

CREATE EQUATIONS FOR KEY TOPICS AND PROCESSES

We're using software and algorithms to make decisions rather than people, which we think is more efficient and scales better.

—Brian Olsavky, Amazon CFO[17]

The hardest part of "doing the math" is getting started. It is a process that requires a deep understanding of your company's operating environment, a talent for math, and a willingness to be transparent—all of which the average person inherently finds reasons to avoid.

It's far easier to spend hours debating subjective reasons for the variances in your operating environment than it is to double down and perfect your equations.

One of the most important things to remember when getting started with the math is to not let the perfect be the enemy of the good. Don't let yourself get hung up on fully optimizing your processes right away. The concept of a fully optimized business process is intimidating for most people. Rather than setting yourself up to give up before you even begin, focus on "doing the math" to drive continuous improvement.

Keeping your eyes on the prize—a key business objective that can improve the customer experience, increase the efficiency of business operations, and scale these impacts financially—is critical to "doing the math."

■ ■ ■

AUGMENTING HUMANS, NOT REPLACING THEM

At the advanced end of IoT-driven businesses are companies using robotics, drones, and autonomous vehicles to improve the efficiency of their businesses. All of these technologies are progressing quickly, moving from the prototype stage to actually driving industry change. But innovation isn't the only thing these technological advances are driving.

They're also driving insecurity and fear—particularly among those worried that robots might take their jobs. There is substance to that worry. A 2016 study from the World Economic Forum estimated that world's fifteen leading countries will lose 5.1 million jobs in the next five years to workplace changes, including artificial intelligence and automation.

But what most people don't understand is that robots, like humans, have certain strengths and weaknesses. Robots are good at simple, repeatable tasks that don't require much dexterity. Humans thrive in creative fields and many manufacturing environments, where their ability to "reprogram themselves" at will allows them to adapt quickly to changes in the process or product. No such luck with robots.

As a result, companies are turning to cobots—robots that can work collaboratively with humans. Amazon uses cobots to scale its fulfillment center processes, relying on technology from Kiva Systems, a robotics company it bought for about $775 million in 2012.

In a traditional warehouse system, employees called pickers walk the floor, picking out items that need to be shipped. Kiva robots actually pick up and deliver the shelves that the picker needs to fulfill the order. Pickers, on the other hand, get to stay mostly put, focusing on fulfillment while the robot does all of the heavy lifting.

Kiva's warehouse bots combine sophisticated sensors, computing power, algorithms, and mechanical design to help fulfill an average of thirty-five orders per second. And warehouse pickers aren't alone—a study out of MIT found that robot-human teams are about 85 percent more effective than either working alone.[18]

■ ■ ■

Principle 5

Think Big, but Start Small

If you double the number of experiments you do per year you're going to double your inventiveness.

—Jeff Bezos[19]

Bezos loves to say that thinking small is a self-fulfilling prophecy. It's no surprise, then, that Amazon's eighth leadership principle, one of the ideas Bezos uses to guide leadership at Amazon, encourages company leaders to think big. (Remember, Amazon's leadership principles are different than the ten principles for successful IoT strategies outlined in this book. For a refresher on the difference, you can revisit my introduction.)

Amazon leadership principle number eight is "Think Big: Leaders create and communicate a bold direction that inspires results. They think differently and look around corners for ways to serve customers."

From revolutionizing online retail to reinventing publishing, the company is known for successfully tackling big opportunities. What many people don't realize is that the key to successfully building these big visions is to start small. That grand vision will guide you all along the way, but in order to get there, you'll need to test your vision—and adjust accordingly—by carrying out lots of little experiments. This is one of the keys to Amazon's innovation and IoT strategies.

Principle 5: Successfully innovating with the Internet of Things requires a big and powerful vision, but to reach that vision, you'll need to create and learn from a series of small, agile experiments.

In this principle, I'll point you toward the processes and strategies you need to get started designing those experiments. The exact steps you'll need to take to create this kind of experimentation within your business or organization will be specific to your circumstances.

Let's start with the obvious—thinking big.

THINKING BIG

In 2002, I launched the third-party business at Amazon, which allowed retailers to sell their products through Amazon's website. Today that business is responsible for more than 50 percent of all units shipped and sold at Amazon. The platform supports more than three million sellers.

As we built the third-party business, we focused on three core principles that would allow it to grow. First, the customer's experience with third-party sellers needed to be as good as when they bought directly from Amazon the retailer. Second, the experience of selling on Amazon's third-party platform had to be intuitive and easy, even though the process was relatively complex. Third, we had to design the platform for and strategize around supporting hundreds of thousands—not tens or hundreds—of sellers.

Because of our strategy, the data and transaction choreography between seller and Amazon had to be more complex. We built tools, examples, test environments, and lots of supports to make selling as intuitive and efficient for sellers as possible. Those tools included three different types of integration paths—XML transactions, which allow more sophisticated sellers to directly connect and automate their product info, inventory, and fulfillment systems; flat-file transactions for sellers who still want machine-to-machine systems integration, but need less sophistication; and a portal-based integration tool where a basic seller could create items and manage orders manually.

Since we were thinking big, we also had to think through topics of scale. Amazon had parity agreements in place with its third-party sellers, requiring them to list items on Amazon at the same price and availability as any other sales channels they might be using. How could we keep track of whether sellers were living up to this obligation?

The most obvious but least scalable and effective option would have been to rely on manual audits or reviews. That would have been an expensive process that only allowed us to review a subset of items. So instead we built an automated system to verify that sellers were living up to their parity obligations. Using the item information they sent us, we were able to crawl their website and any other sales channels to verify the consistency of their pricing and availability.

Having and holding a big vision for creating an outstanding customer and seller experience was critical in laying the foundation for success.

All of this was us thinking big.

But don't confuse "thinking big" with "betting big." The business and art of innovation lie in the many failures—the learning, adjusting, and moving ahead—that come along the way. The principle you'll find below the waterline is about how to scale failure.

STARTING SMALL

The better you become at creating ways to fail repeatedly in small ways, the more likely you are to achieve big success. In other words, think big, but act small.

It took years before the third-party business became the force that it is today. Before I even joined the marketplace team, Amazon had already tried—and failed—to build two other third-party seller platforms. Amazon Auctions iterated to Z-Shops, which iterated to Marketplace. The first two were failures; the third is now a huge success.

And although Amazon certainly invested in the Marketplace business, it was not a high-risk investment. Instead leadership invested in relatively small individual experiments that would improve Amazon's long-term understanding of the winning formula.

What do those smaller experiments look like? At Marketplace, we thought up front that customers would want to shop through seller-specific storefronts, so we built out the infrastructure for sellers to create branded online storefronts. Once we actually launched storefronts, though, we found customers were actually more likely to shop by category across Amazon's entire site. As a result, we wound up deemphasizing merchant-specific storefronts and focusing instead on improving Amazon's core browsing and searching capabilities.

It wasn't until Marketplace eventually found the right long-term formula—through this and many other experiments—that the company shifted its focus to growth.

These are two of the traits of successful innovators: They execute on lots of small experiments, and they hold a patient, long-term approach to product and business success. It is rare, though not impossible, that innovation and short-term profits go together.

When a company is developing IoT capabilities, these ideas become even more important.

GETTING SMALL IN YOUR BUSINESS

Executed well, these kinds of small experiments help you understand your customer's needs and how your product might fit the market. Executed poorly, they can be worse than not experimenting at all.

A failed experiment could just as easily be the result of bad execution as it could a valid test of your hypothesis about a product.

Luckily, Amazon and others have developed tactics for acting small and moving iteratively to help you avoid this trap.

Low-fidelity prototyping. If you've ever created something that only partially works just to test a few critical components, you've created a low-fidelity prototype. Google's Cardboard is an example of a low-fidelity virtual-reality prototype: By sticking their phones inside a VR viewer made out of cardboard, users can test and experiment with VR. The first version of this was likely hacked together with a few off-the-shelf parts and a cardboard box. Meanwhile, Google is using Cardboard to build out its developer community and to test the popularity of virtual reality without spending valuable time and money developing a more complex VR product.

From an IoT perspective, think about ways you can test the effectiveness or viability of adding sensors to a product without actually building it out. This could mean strapping sensors onto a physical product rather than hardwiring them in. Low-fidelity prototyping can be useful as a visual demonstration of how a product might work and as a way to build buy-in for a full prototype development.

Minimum Viable Product. The idea of a minimum viable product, or MVP, was popularized by Eric Ries's 2011 book, *The Lean Startup*, which encouraged business owners to identify and test the critical assumptions behind their businesses and solutions. Ries, inspired by the work of his mentor, Steve Blank, popularized the idea of using a minimum viable version of your product to help you prove or disprove assumptions about your business and customers through carefully constructed trials.

Functioning prototypes. Once you've used low-fidelity prototypes to test some of your early assumptions, it may be time to build a functional prototype or early working version of your product. Unlike your MVP, which generally includes little technical development, your prototype is generally used as the technical basis for your product. These can still be incomplete in many ways—an early version to drive future iteration—but you will want to be sure you're working from a solid basis for future full-throated product development.

Fail Fast, and Fail Forward. Building a team that can make the most of its failures—and that knows how to create new learning for itself—comes down to one thing: encouraging smart, quick failure. Your job is to make sure your team understands the difference between a failure that drives learning and a failure of execution. The first gives you valuable data. The second only wastes your time.

GETTING COMFORTABLE WITH SMALL FAILURES

"One area where I think we are especially distinctive," Bezos wrote in Amazon's 2015 shareholder letter, "is failure. I believe we are the best place in the world to fail (we have plenty of practice!), and failure and invention are inseparable twins. To invent you have to experiment, and if you know in advance that it's going to work, it's not an experiment. Most large organizations embrace the idea of invention, but are not willing to suffer the string of failed experiments necessary to get there."[20]

Amazon's most prolific failure was the Fire Phone, launched in July of 2014. It was a short-lived market miss that resulted in a $170-million inventory write-off.

"What the hell happened with the Fire Phone?" Henry Blodget, the famous stock analyst, asked Jeff Bezos in a *Business Insider* discussion.

Jeff's response that day came down to this: the Fire Phone, like all of Amazon's projects, was an experiment. In Jeff's mind, its failure was a learning experience—another chance to iterate or pivot. The phone, Jeff explained, was just one more entry in Amazon's "device portfolio"—with "portfolio" being the operative word.

As a leader in the IoT space, Jeff views every project as an investment in Amazon's portfolio. And yes, he has diversified.

"It's early," he said, "and we've had a lot of things we've had to iterate on at Amazon. One of my jobs as the leader at Amazon is to encourage people to be bold," he explained; "to create a shield around the teams innovating so they can focus on the hard things they are accomplishing and minimize the noise and concerns of detractors within the company."[21]

As Amazon launched its next round of smart devices, we saw them resorting to their standard playbook: launch a product or service quickly, don't make too big of deal of it, and spend almost nothing on marketing. Instead, get customer feedback and make adjustments or cut quickly. Launch more experiments.

The Amazon Echo was an invitation-only product for Amazon Prime customers. It was advertised as a "beta" product and in limited edition, keeping expectations low and company learning high. It followed the same playbook for the Dash and Dash Button. Only when feedback and reviews of the Echo and Dash Button were fantastic did Amazon open them up to the public.

This is the role of the IoT leader. It's also the reason Amazon is leading the way into the IoT space.

CAN YOU COACH SPEED?

What's incredible about Amazon is that it innovates and scales so aggressively, while also leveraging operational excellence across its supply chain. It has made a name for itself on predictability—as an Amazon customer, you know when your order ships, how long it will take to arrive, and that Amazon Web Services outages will be resolved as quickly as humanly possible. Amazon has done this by focusing on ruthless efficiency and discipline.

These are the same traits that can make it hard to create an environment of innovation, where experimentation, breaking from industry norms, figuring out new partnership scenarios, and potentially cannibalizing existing businesses are encouraged.

That's why Gartner recently ranked Amazon the number one supply-chain company in the world—because of its singular ability to be world class at both operational excellence *and* innovation. Gartner calls this ability "bimodal" and explains it as "an environment where business models must change quickly, where the expectation is that they will spend as much or more time growing and innovating as they will streamlining and promoting efficiency."[22]

There's a common belief in sports that you can't coach speed; you are either born fast, or you weren't. Training and technique can develop, hone, and refine that speed, but nothing can make a slow athlete fast.

Most teams and companies are the same when it comes to being innovative. Take the *Fortune* 1000, a list of top companies stack ranked by revenue. Churn among the *Fortune* 1000 has accelerated pretty rapidly over the years—from 35 percent in the 1970s to more than 70 percent in the 2000s. Hold out your ten fingers. If each of those fingers represents a company in the *Fortune* 1000, eight of those fingers will be replaced over the next decade. In most cases, that's the direct result of an inability or lack of will to innovate.

How do you keep from becoming a victim of churn? The Internet of Things provides a unique opportunity for companies to leverage their established products, services, and channels; create new value for customers; and build innovation in their businesses. It just might be the best basis to build speed ever presented.

The key to doing this successfully, though, is finding the right leaders. Finding leaders with the critical eye and instincts necessary to identify and execute on this kind of opportunity is tough—it's a magical skill set.

As innovation researcher Maxwell Wessel wrote in *Harvard Business Review*,

> When corporations reach maturity, the measure of success is very different: its profit. Once a business figures out how to solve its customers' problems, organizational structures and processes emerge to guide the company towards efficient operation. Seasoned managers steer their employees from pursuing the art of discovery and towards engaging in the science of delivery. Employees are taught to seek efficiencies, leverage existing assets and distribution channels, and listen to (and appease) their best customers.
>
> Such practices and policies ensure that executives can deliver meaningful earnings to the street and placate shareholders. But they also minimize the types and scale of innovation that can be pursued successfully within an organization. No company ever created a transformational growth product by asking: "How can we do what we're already doing, a tiny bit better and a tiny bit cheaper?"[23]

In other words, asking the same teams and people to be both operators and innovators will fail.

The two things a company leader (be that CEO or middle manager) is best positioned to do are to communicate vision and allocate resources. For enterprises to combine operational excellence and systematically create innovation, to help give permission to move quickly and "fail forward," leaders must create the environment to nurture tiny seeds.

"Both [Amazon Retail and AWS]," Bezos explained, "were planted as tiny seeds and both have grown organically...one is famous for brown boxes and the other for APIs...under the surface, the two are not so different. They share a distinctive organizational culture that cares deeply about and acts with conviction on a small number of principles." Those principles, as designed by company leadership, have created the scaffolding for a culture of forward failure that carries success across Amazon's many lines of business.

The key to innovation, within Amazon or your own company, is to imagine and build your own scaffolding of trial and error. "You need to select people who tend to be dissatisfied by a lot of the current ways," explains Bezos. "As they go about their daily experiences, they notice that little things are broken in the world and they want to fix them. Inventors have a divine discontent...you want to embrace high-judgment failure—this was worth trying, it didn't work, so let's try something different. All of our most important successes at Amazon have been through that kind of failure: Fail, try again, and repeat that loop."[24]

HOW TO GET YOUR ELEPHANT TO DANCE

How does Amazon consistently build this *bimodal* capability? How to get large companies, the elephants, to continue to consistently innovate is a question for the ages. But if you've studied Amazon like I have, you'll realize that there are a few tricks and approaches that can help an elephant—or any other company—innovate, particularly when it comes to the Internet of Things.

1. *Invest Like a Venture Capital Firm, and Create a New Portfolio.* Many companies squash innovation and invention because they want predictable results—predictable timeframe, predictable

investment, predictable financial returns. This is how a private equity company invests.

There are times in IoT where this is the right mentality. When you're improving and automating an internal process, for example, you should have a good idea of what the returns and risks are. But when you're creating new, innovative customer features or developing new IoT business lines, your investments, risks, and returns will be harder to predict. In this case, the job of a successful IoT leader is to act like a venture-capital firm. The key is a balanced portfolio, understanding the differences between different segments of your investment portfolio. Many of your IoT customer facing and business model investments are going to be high risk. For high risk investments, they need to be small experiments to prove out key aspects before scaling. Think big, but act small.

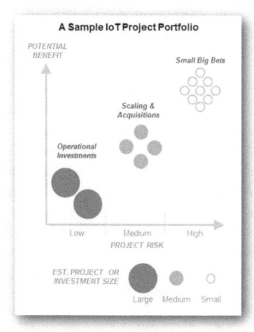

2. *Create Autonomy and Separation.* To create significant departure and disruption from current business practices, the teams within your company that are dedicated to creating innovation

need to be separated from the teams representing the status quo. In Amazon's case, the company has built a special team called Lab126 that is focused only on creating innovation in their devices. Tellingly, that team is based in California, far from the company's Seattle base.

While separation is key, so is direct, unfiltered communication and collaboration with a company's CEO or senior leader. Jeff Bezos is often referred to as "chief product officer" for projects. It is his job to keep that team insulated while maintaining detailed collaboration and visibility with senior leadership.

3. *Dedicate a Senior, Capable Leader to the Initiative.* At many companies, you can identify a leader's cachet by the headcount and expense budget he or she manages. Not so much at Amazon, where senior people are often dedicated to leading new big bets. Take, for example, Steve Kessel, the longtime executive who launched the first Kindle. Kessel's latest project is Amazon's nascent retail-store initiative, the first of which just launched in Seattle.[25]

Jeff and Amazon believe there's added power in opening up key teams and leaders to focus on something new. The critical word we used at Amazon was "obsession"—let a top leader obsess about his or her objectives. If the initiative is just one of the teams and objectives that leader manages, it won't possibly benefit from the level of obsession that complete dedication brings.

4. *Craft the Right Metrics and Goals. Hint: They're Not Typically about Profit.* One of the things I remember most about my time at Amazon was the company's intense focus on solidifying a new initiative's metrics and goals. Long before a new project launched, the team behind it would outline its goals—whether growth, operational performance, customer experience, or costs—and create a set of metrics to measure those goals over time. The idea was that if we got the goals and metrics right, the team could succeed with more independence and less governance. That

independence also leads to more creativity, as team members found creative ways to meet those goals.

5. *Integrated Multidisciplinary Teams.* Amazon has two rules of thumb for building teams they can count on to think and act innovatively. The first is to create a team composed of people with a variety of disciplines and backgrounds. Unique ideas and the ability to execute on them usually stem from teams that can think broadly. Working in the Internet of Things, capabilities in user experience, industrial design, user-interface design, business-model design, and data science are especially useful.

   The second rule of thumb is to focus on small teams: Amazon often quantifies this as a "two-pizza team." In other words, you should be able to feed your whole team with two pizzas. That means no more than eight people. Two-pizza teams not only own a capability, but they're responsible for everything from market definition and product roadmap to building and operations.

6. *Create an Insanely Better Product or Service.* In the end, the result and by-product of the above ingredients has to yield an insanely good product or service. This is not just a marginal improvement. It is not a completely new but still average product. Successful innovation results in an incredible experience, at the right price point. It surprises users, and it very quickly becomes indispensable to your customers.

You'll remember at the beginning of this book that we talked about the IoT triple threat—the idea that you can use IoT to (1) improve customer experiences, (2) improve and streamline operations, and (3) develop new business models. If you're clever about strategy, you can do all three of these things with one move.

At this point in the book, we've talked about using IoT to make customer experiences better and to integrate those experiences across platforms and services. We've also covered how IoT can help you make operational improvements in your business or organization.

In the coming chapters, we'll talk about the third part of the triple threat—the business models that can be powered by IoT. Many companies will start their IoT journey by focusing on the first two parts of the triple threat, but if you plan ahead, you can actually build in the flexibility that will allow you to take advantage of IoT-driven business models.

Even if you're not planning to implement a new business model at this time, understanding how they work can create more flexibility for you and your business and open more doors down the line.

Principle 6

How to Become a Platform Business Using the Internet of Things

When a platform is self-service, even improbable ideas
get tried, because there's no expert gatekeeper ready to
say "That will never work!" Guess what?
Many of those improbable ideas do work.

—Jeff Bezos, 2011 Letter to Shareholders

Imagine for a moment that you own a business that provides a service to your community, a market, or an industry. To make your service the best in the world, you also design, build, test, and use innovative tools and capabilities that not only make your business better but can be sold to other businesses. Your business gets bigger and bigger because your service gets better and better, and your innovative tools become more and more in demand. It's a virtuous circle.

In other words, you've become a platform company—your platform and the innovative tools you build are your service.

Principle 6: Building a platform business model, which allows others to leverage your capabilities to build and grow their own businesses, creates a stronger sustainable, competitive advantage for

your business. The Internet of Things creates exciting possibilities for companies to develop a platform business model, leveraging their connected devices for other companies use.

In this chapter, we'll explore how Amazon identifies, tests, and builds its own potential platform businesses using IoT, how to figure out if a platform business model might be right for you, and how to think about using the Internet of Things to build your platform business model.

Building platform businesses is the Amazon way. It's the reason Amazon.com currently sells more goods online than its next twelve biggest competitors combined, including Walmart, Apple, Macy's, and Target.[26] It's a major reason why Amazon sales are growing faster than Internet sales as a whole, accounting for more than 50 percent of all US e-commerce revenue growth. On the enterprise side, it's a huge reason that Amazon Web Services (AWS) leads the cloud-computing market in size, innovation, and mind share.

The Amazon Marketplace platform powers many of Amazon's retail capabilities and core assets and enables millions of third parties to sell and deliver items to customers. Amazon's retail business needed scalable technology infrastructure and tools. It turns out other businesses needed the flexible technology infrastructure as well, and the Amazon Web Services (AWS) cloud business was formed, serving both Amazon the retailer and thousands of other clients.

Now Amazon sees an opportunity for an Internet of Things platform. Enter Alexa, poised to become Amazon's Trojan horse for IoT.

Through Alexa, the Internet of Things is developing as yet another platform business for Amazon. I expect it to expand for them in much the same way that AWS and Marketplace have. Already Alexa is a voice-controlled interactive platform leveraged by thousands of other companies. This is good news for you because Amazon and other IoT platforms can fuel your IoT plans. These companies also create a model for how to build an IoT platform business.

Not every company has what it takes to build a platform—but if you're interested in getting your feet wet, there are a few questions you should ask yourself before diving in.

What does it mean to be a platform business? How does it relate to IoT? Where is the opportunity? Let's explore…

SIMPLIFICATION EPITOMIZED: AMAZON'S PLATFORM BUSINESSES

Traditional businesses tend to offer a core capability and value proposition to a customer and then organize capabilities to meet that customer's needs. Take Warby Parker, which makes private-label glasses and sells them online and in their stores, direct to consumer. They sell specific goods—stylish prescription glasses at a great price—that are easy to try on and return, simplifying the glasses-purchasing process.

Platform businesses, on the other hand, create the fundamental capabilities for customers and traditional businesses to do business with one another. They may provide some products or services themselves, but for the most part, they rely heavily on other parties to supply the goods offered to customers. iTunes, which allows artists to upload and sell their songs to customers, is an example of that. Artists direct their fans to the platform, creating a network effect that builds the value of iTunes itself—another hallmark of a platform business.

Platforms knit together complex processes and tasks that are normally more complex for both suppliers and consumers. Amazon's third-party merchant platform is successful because it makes the process of setting up an online shop, building access to customers, and fulfilling orders—which would normally be complicated and expensive—seamless for small businesses. At the same time, it makes comparison shopping and purchasing seamless and trustworthy for consumers.

In its ideal state, a platform's capabilities can also be extended and improved upon by other technology developers and other companies. Earlier in this book, we talked about some of the third-party businesses developing software and other capabilities for Amazon's Echo. As third parties innovate on a platform, those companies and businesses transition from acting as traditional suppliers or vendors to being partners in the business. This is a major advantage of running a successful platform business—you benefit from other partners innovating on the services and capabilities you provide.

Some platform businesses not only let partners use and innovate on services or capabilities, but they allow them to embed these capabilities in other products and services. Take PayPal, which allows users to send and receive money on its platform but also allows sellers to embed PayPal payment processing directly into their own websites. Or take the iTunes App Store, which allows third-party developers to create new capabilities for Apple phones. Alexa Voice Service can be used in other products as the software powering the voice-activated device.

When you enable and incentivize other businesses to build on your capabilities, you are crowdsourcing ideas, innovation, and investment to the betterment of your capabilities.

PLATFORMS -- THE AMAZON WAY

A "platform" is a system that can be programmed and therefore customized by outside developers—users—and in that way, adapted to countless needs and niches that the platform's original developers could not have possibly contemplated, much less had time to accommodate.[27]

—MARC ANDREESSEN

When I was at Amazon in the early 2000s, we developed the concept that Amazon was fundamentally two types of businesses. First, it was an online retailer selling everything from books to shampoo. Second, though, it was a platform business that built capabilities for outside companies. Those capabilities were used by Amazon the retailer as well as other companies.

I ran two of Amazon's platform businesses: First, I launched and scaled the third-party Marketplace business, which today is responsible for more than 50 percent of all units shipped and sold through Amazon. Second, I ran the Enterprise Services business, which ran other large retailers' e-commerce infrastructures for them, including website infrastructure and management software and branded fulfillment and customer service. Target.com, Toys "R" Us, Marks & Spencer, Sears Canada, and the NBA have all used Amazon's Enterprise Services platform.

As I worked to build those businesses for Amazon, I was following four clear rules for successful platform business.

1. *Platforms Should Simplify Complexity.* The first rule of thumb is that you should build a platform business to make hard things simple, often making them self-service. Rather than trying to support confusing or complicated tools with lots of account support required, teams focused on building services that were ridiculously obvious and easy to use. In addition to creating better user experiences and products, this approach provides major benefits to a platform's ability to scale—adding more users does not directly require more headcount to manage them. Doing this right means making hard things simple and accessible to the right audiences. "Someone shouldn't have to talk to you to use your stuff," was a common refrain among Amazon leadership.

2. *Platforms Use APIs to Make Embedding Easy for Customers.* A platform should be made programmable by creating an application programming interface, or API. Think of an API as a well-defined set of requirements for how one software program talks to another. Creating an API makes technology integration—the use of your platform by other companies—simple and feasible at scale.

3. *Platforms Provide Ongoing Value.* To create a sustaining platform business, there needs to be an ongoing value proposition that the platform provides and protects. For the Amazon Marketplace

business, the heart of this was protecting customer trust by providing payment and account services and extending the A-to-Z
Guarantee to third-party products and protecting third-party
trust by providing customer demand.

4. *Eat Your Own Dog Food.* As was the case with AWS, Amazon
generally builds its platform businesses just as much for internal
customers—Amazon Prime or e-commerce teams, for example—
as for external customers. Amazon Retail runs on AWS infrastructure, and many of the innovations of AWS—scaling, reliability
requirements, security requirements, and international capabilities—have come from having to support such a massive retail
business. Products take lessons from Amazon's early and exacting
internal users to drive R&D and scale much more quickly.

Examples of platforms that Amazon has built and operates today include
the following:

- *Amazon Web Services.* As we mentioned above, AWS is the leading cloud-computing-innovation company. In case you've been
hiding in a computer closet for the last ten years, its diverse set
of on-demand infrastructure, data management, and solutions
make up a $10 billion business annually, with operating margins
greater than 20 percent. It also happens to be growing at more
than 60 percent year over year.

- *Fulfillment by Amazon.* Fulfillment by Amazon, known as FBA,
allows sellers and companies to use Amazon warehouses to
store inventory and fulfill orders (sold either on Amazon.com or
through other websites). Thousands of small and medium-sized
companies use Amazon's more than three hundred worldwide
fulfillment centers to store and ship goods, giving them a global
distribution network they could only dream about. Over one billion items were shipped by Amazon on behalf of third-party sellers in 2015.[28]

- *Amazon Machine Learning.* Machine learning can be extremely technically complicated, based on complex algorithms and technology. But Amazon's machine learning service gives developers at all levels a set of visualizations and wizards to help walk them through the process of creating machine learning models. This platform was first developed as part of Amazon's internal machine learning capabilities, then turned into an external service.
- *Amazon Marketplace.* As we mentioned above, Amazon Marketplace accounts for more than 50 percent of all units sold at Amazon. The key to Marketplace's success was threefold— we didn't compromise on the buying experience for customers shopping with third parties; we created a simple, intuitive seller experience despite the complex integration and set of choreography and data required between the seller and Amazon; and we built a seamless combination of Amazon Prime, Amazon FBA, and Amazon Marketplace that really drove growth.
- *CreateSpace.* Amazon's self-service, on-demand publishing platform lets authors like me easily write, design, and publish books. It facilitates print and e-book distribution without authors having to go through the traditional-publishing-house gatekeepers. It was an easy decision for me to self-publish through CreateSpace rather than go through a traditional publisher. One huge advantage is Amazon's on-demand printing capability. I often speak in front of audiences and teams, which requires a large book order. With CreateSpace, I can order the books I want just a few days in advance rather than having to order large batches with several weeks of lead time.

The examples cover some of Amazon's most substantial platform businesses, but Amazon is also developing and incubating a host of smaller platform businesses. Amazon Video Direct, which lets users upload and profit from professional-grade video content, is an embryotic platform business that could someday grow into a huge business like the others.

Mechanical Turk is a platform to outsource small tasks to a worldwide labor pool.

As Bezos wrote in the 2011 shareholder letter, "The most radical and transformative of inventions are often those that empower others to unleash their creativity—to pursue their dreams. That's a big part of what's going on with Amazon Web Services, Fulfillment by Amazon, and Kindle Direct Publishing. With AWS, FBA, and KDP, we are creating powerful self-service platforms that allow thousands of people to boldly experiment and accomplish things that would otherwise be impossible or impractical. These innovative, large-scale platforms are not zero-sum—they create win-win situations and create significant value for developers, entrepreneurs, customers, authors, and readers."[2]

Amazon's business platforms are enablers. They enable writers and booksellers and small business owners. They enable developers and IT professionals to focus on adding business value rather than worrying about technology infrastructure. Amazon platforms enable businesses to outsource labor and empower entrepreneurs to pursue personal and professional growth.

And all of the energy it creates eventually comes back. The virtuous cycles of Amazon business platforms circulate and expand energy just like the Amazon flywheel itself.

THE ECHO: AMAZON'S IOT TROJAN HORSE

Amazon's Echo looks simple enough—it's a cylinder-shaped consumer electronic device, sleek, dark, and unassuming. Don't be taken in. That trim black exterior is just the pretty face on a bundle of features, each designed to enable the Internet of Things.

With its sophisticated form—a seven-microphone array, subwoofer and tweeter speakers, advanced voice-recognition software, remote control, and onboard computer with processors, memory, and power supply—even the earliest version of the Echo seemed to early adopters an innovative gadget for their home. They could ask Alexa all kinds of convenient things. Things like,

- "Alexa, play my country playlist."
- "Alexa, what is the weather forecast?"
- "Alexa, add Gatorade to my shopping list."

Over the past year, the Alexa teams have continued to add to her list of skills, with over one thousand skills built by other companies and developers. Alexa's integration with third-party devices and services is growing exponentially:

- "Alexa, arrange an Uber to the Seattle airport."
- "Alexa, tell Garage.io to close the garage door."
- "Alexa, how much gas is in my Ford car?"

The teams behind Alexa and Echo are constantly working with third-party vendors like Uber, Garage.io, and Ford to add integrations with their products. Each of these third-party applications can be downloaded to and managed through your Echo.

It takes coordination to integrate each of these new capabilities. Within Amazon's organizational structure, Echo is composed of several hardware teams (to create both internal and external device hardware), several software teams, and several partner teams to create these external relationships with partners. Each of these teams has its own independent strategy, product roadmap, business plan, and adoption scenario. And each of these teams is actively coordinating with the strategies, roadmaps, business plans, and adoption scenarios of Echo's other teams.

Watching the growth of Echo's "talents" over the last year, it has become clear that, in Amazon's mind, the Echo is far more than just an interactive home speaker. To Amazon, it's a new type of computing interface that helps customers interface with their connected devices.

Think of Echo as Amazon's first Internet of Things PC. It's a computing device that performs calculations and beams queries to your connected devices, but instead of a keyboard and mouse acting as the primary interface, it uses voice for input and sound for output. And if Echo is Amazon's connection to the Internet of Things, the bridge between home and Internet, then Alexa herself becomes much more than just a disembodied voice spouting facts and playing music.

Alexa is Amazon's first hands-free operating system.

THE SECRET SAUCE

When Echo launched in 2015 as a plug-in, always-on listening device, it was the only device using Alexa. Since then, Amazon has introduced the Tap, a portable battery-operated version of the Echo, and the Dot, a smaller Alexa interface. There are rumors also of a voice-activated Kindle tablet on the way.

In the end, though, all of these devices are really just the container for Amazon's secret sauce—Alexa.

At its simplest, Alexa provides three critical capabilities:

1. *Sophisticated Speech-Recognition Capabilities.* Similar to Apple's Siri, Alexa Voice Services allows connected devices like Echo to recognize and assign meaning to users' vocal commands. Alexa Voice Services uses cloud computing and machine learning to improve its recognition capabilities based on individual interactions with users. And, much like Google Search uses machine learning to improve itself with each use, Alexa Voice Services pools its learning across all users to improve user interactions and the accuracy of search results.

2. *Event Triggering.* Alexa provides event recognition, a rules engine, and the technology interface to run third-party applications. At Amazon, each custom application is referred to as a skill. For example, an Uber skill allows a user to request an Uber ride. There is a combination of tools built by Amazon to enable this event recognition capability, but it essentially consists of defining a keyword to trigger your skill, a set of voice-command keywords, such as "start" or "order," and then a list of rules on what to do or

what to return. There are hundreds of third-party skills available today, and the platform is just getting started.

3. *Software Platform for Voice Interaction and Integration.* Finally, Alexa can be used as a software platform on other products, similar in nature to an operating system. Amazon allows other companies to download and license the Alexa software and use it on their own devices and products for free.

Along with all of this, Amazon has created an investment fund, the Alexa Fund, providing "up to $100 million" to help developers, manufacturers, and startups build new voice-driven technologies and applications using Alexa's developer tools and APIs.[29] All types of companies, products, and services can embed Alexa into their products.

"We've made adding Alexa incredibly easy for developers," said Greg Hart, vice president of Amazon Echo and Alexa Voice Services. "Any device with a speaker, an Internet connection, and a microphone can integrate Alexa with just a few lines of code. From startups to established companies, we can't wait to see how developers integrate Alexa."[30]

What can companies do with this? Toymail uses Alexa Voice Services (AVS) as the technical backbone and operating system for toys that allow kids to send and receive voice messages. Scout Alarm uses AVS for voice control and integration in their connected home-security system.

What is Amazon's motivation or rationale for giving Alexa away? They're making a long-term bet on the development of Alexa: they're betting that they can get other companies to develop Alexa's skills and to use Alexa as the voice-recognition system in their products—that Alexa will become a major platform for devices that use voice interaction and event triggering, which, as it turns out, is a large segment of IoT scenarios.

Alexa is a Trojan horse. It's a Trojan horse that creates many opportunities.

First, like the Amazon Dash, Alexa (via the Echo device) provides customers with a direct line to Amazon product purchases. The more customers that use Alexa, the more product purchases Amazon will see.

Second, Alexa will be most natively integrated into AWS, a fact that will drive the consumption of a remarkable amount of storage, computing, network bandwidth, and other higher-end cloud capabilities. At the moment, as it incubates and supports its new ecosystem, Amazon is paying for the computing costs Alexa incurs on AWS infrastructure. Down the line, though, as the ecosystem grows more and more robust, they will likely start working with application providers to charge for consumption of AWS services. (We'll talk about this more in principle 10.)

Third, both Alexa's voice-recognition and search-processing capabilities are built using machine learning. Machine learning requires more data to learn. That means that the more consumers use Alexa, the better the results will be—much like Google Search, which increases its accuracy and value with each new piece of history and context. So, in these early days of voice-recognition capability, it is critical to become the market leader and drive improvement through use.

THE IOT PLATFORM OPPORTUNITY

What can other companies take from this IoT platform strategy? Other than "consider using Alexa as your voice-recognition software solution" (this is not a trivial suggestion!), the potential is this: building connected devices could be a Trojan horse for becoming the embedded infrastructure for your customers. You have a chance to build a platform that is valuable for other companies to participate and leverage your connected devices in ways you could monetize.

When you become the operating infrastructure, your products become much harder to replace. Your partners will teach you a tremendous amount about the usage and problems of your product and services. Your revenue model will likely be accretive and recurring. And when your product and capabilities can be "programmed" into environments, likely through an API, the cost of replacement skyrockets. Ripping and replacing programmed infrastructure is hard and expensive.

Of course, Amazon isn't alone in recognizing the power of platform. Apple, Facebook, and Google have all leveraged some variation with similar traits. Together, Apple, Facebook, Google, and Amazon have come to be known as the Gang of Four. As Eric Schmidt commented, "It seems to me that there are four companies that are exploiting platform strategies really well."[31]

Among these, consumer-based platform strategies—like the Apple App Store and Facebook—are easiest to recognize. But business-to-business (B2B) platforms, though fewer, present more opportunity.

In B2B industries, there will be many opportunities to create unique platforms within the realm of IoT based simply on where your company's products are already located and how they're already being used.

A company that manufactures and installs hand dryers, for example, could leverage the physical position of its equipment to create a platform for monitoring and serving bathrooms and patrons. Example scenarios could include notifying cleaning teams of needed supply replacements, reordering supplies themselves, and providing security services. The maintenance ecosystem could leverage the "hand-dryer platform" to monitor water on the floor to avoid slip-and-fall situations. Video monitoring, voice and event identification, and other data sensors, all potentially positioned from the physical unit, could be valuable to many other companies.

You now have a platform.

Bigbelly, a trash-equipment company, is already building out an IoT platform strategy around another unglamorous but huge opportunity—garbage cans. By thinking in concentric circles, Bigbelly has created a better municipal and public trash receptacle—solar-powered sensors monitor capacity and supply power to a compactor, which creates up to eight times more capacity. This has also allowed Bigbelly to add new services and revenue opportunities—a "clean management system" provides real-time data to drive operational improvements and serves as a platform for an ecosystem of additional services. Security and Wi-Fi hotspots are two early use cases.

This pattern of leveraging infrastructure to allow others to access, operate, and extend their services is the same platform strategy Amazon has repeatedly used to innovate and gain scale.

But this is so much more than a technical and architecture question. The most common mistake companies and leaders make is thinking that platforms are, at their core, a technology challenge.

As Phil Simon wrote in *The Age of the Platform*, "An overall mind-set based on openness and third party collaboration is absolutely essential in building a true platform. That mentality is much more important than any individual API or technology."[32]

How to monetize? How to partner and build the ecosystem? How to operate and update the infrastructure? How to manage risk and liability? How to provide high availability? How to do updates? How to manage security? A successful platform play will need to address all of these and more.

IoT is providing this set of opportunities to many more companies going forward, as each device category opens up a new set of scenarios. Amazon is positioning the Echo to be the house IoT platform, car brands around the world are maneuvering to become the auto IoT platform, and GE is turning the aircraft carrier to become the industrial IoT platform. But there are many more IoT platform opportunities, essentially each unique operations or physical domain—buildings, bathrooms, emergency rooms, basketballs, delivery trucks, even shoes.

Any device that is in a situation that is a good "perch," or crow's nest, for monitoring, collecting data and events, and allowing other entities to leverage (and pay) for the access to that perch is potentially in a position to become a platform.

That being said, though, building a platform will only be the right strategy for a minority of companies. Becoming a platform is yet another big change to add on top of the transitions needed to move from a product company to an IoT-enabled service company.

ARE YOU IN A GOOD POSITION TO BECOME A PLATFORM COMPANY?

As you consider whether your company might benefit from investing in the infrastructure and services it takes to create an IoT-based platform, evaluate the following.

1. *Location and Positioning of Product.* The location and positioning of your product or company assets can determine the strategic nature of the data and events that could be captured. Do you have a "perch"? A well-positioned product provides a valuable crow's nest, whereas a product with narrow visibility has less potential to act as a platform. Positioning is also a big determinant to the connectivity options available to the device, which impacts both costs and the amount, speed, and reliability of data connection and transport.

2. *Form Factor of Product.* Does the form factor of your product provide a basis for integrating other sensors and the associated infrastructure? Could your device allow for other sensors to be located on it? Incumbents, because of their install base and industry relationships, can have an advantage here, but their success should not be taken for granted. Look at connected-home startups like Nest and Scout as companies that are disrupting incumbents.

3. *Technology Chops.* What's your pedigree or your interest in being a technology company? You will become a software and technology company if you decide to proceed with a platform strategy. This is a major strategy decision that should include many considerations. Should the platform be generally "open" or "closed" with a limited number of partners?

4. *Operating Environment Complexity.* You now have to operate a high-availability platform within a complex ecosystem. When an issue happens or a software update needs to be made to a device, that adds complexity to testing and release. Data-sharing

rights, security, updates, and reporting will all need to be added to your list of operating considerations.

5. *Play the Long Game or the Short Game?* Becoming a successful platform company typically requires playing the long game. It takes time and investment to build competencies like testing platforms, APIs, and developer engagement. It takes time to drive customer adoption and use of the platform. If you're a company that needs to find short-term, revenue-generating wins, becoming a platform may not be the strategy for you.

Old-school technology people are likely familiar with the acronym SMOP—"simple matter of programming." Typically used as an ironic response to "All you need to do is program the technology to accomplish blah," SMOP points out that it is always more complex than just "programming the capability." Perhaps SMOP needs to stand for "simple matter of (being a) platform." Being a platform company may sound like "just develop the software, and make it available," but becoming a platform company, or releasing IoT products that you want others to build on and integrate with, is much more complicated than just a SMOP.

In my first book, I wrote a section called "The Critical Capabilities of a Platform Company," which gives a framework for thinking through the implications of becoming a platform company. Business-model implications, operational implications, ecosystem implications, and a baseline set of critical capabilities that a platform likely needs to provide are outlined. For example, a critical capability a platform needs to provide is to help manage data and content in a trusted manner.

For traditional product and service companies evaluating making an IoT platform, these considerations hold true. The best IoT use cases flow across multiple products and typically across multiple enterprises. The prior discussed example, Audi, DHL, and Amazon have partnered in Germany to enable a package to be delivered to the trunk of your car. Structuring and operating ongoing partnerships like this is complex and vital for compelling IoT capabilities, and the skills to build these partnerships put a premium on "partnership" capabilities in organizations that may traditionally not have partnerships like this. Partnership capability will be an organizational muscle that is developed for IoT business to flourish.

As has been and will be throughout this book, "think big, but start small" is the ethos that innovators and companies becoming innovators will adopt. So get going on your IoT platform strategy!

Principle 7

The Outcome-Based Business Model

I've worked in the project-management business essentially my entire career, leading teams of people to accomplish focused, specific objectives driven by a business opportunity. Whether at Amazon or in my consulting practice, solving problems and launching new products or capabilities can be incredibly energizing.

Along the way, I've learned that my favorite word in the English language is "done." It's especially gratifying when it's preceded or followed by the word "well." "Well done" is a powerful phrase. Something is complete; it's packaged; it meets expectations; it's independent; and you get to move on to the next item. "Well done'" is what my clients hire me for.

But there is something even more important, and that is the intended result of "done"—an outcome.

Outcome-based models transition companies from selling a product or service through a transaction to providing what the customer is truly seeking—an outcome.

What exactly does that mean? If you're a music lover, you care less about the specifics of the machine playing your music than you do about its outcome—an endless selection of high-quality music in your pocket. If you need transportation, you care less about whether or not you own your specific vehicle than about the outcome of owning that vehicle— that you have affordable, reliable transportation whenever you need it.

Lastly, if you're a small business owner, you probably don't feel particularly attached to the idea of owning a data center and all of the employees and infrastructure providing the technology infrastructure. You do want highly scalable computer power that you pay for only when you use it.

Welcome to the outcome-based economy.

Principle 7: Connected devices facilitate the creation of outcome-based businesses, an innovative model in which customers pay for the results a product or service provides rather than the product or service itself, shifting ownership, effectiveness, and maintenance responsibilities back to the provider and aligning customer and provider interests.

In this chapter, I'll explain how the Internet of Things facilitates outcome-based business models. We'll also explore the differences between the three types of outcome-based business models—self-service monitoring products, subscription, and as-a-service. I'll also explain how the Internet of Things should be integrated with each and explore whether an outcome-based model might be right for you.

Outcome-based business models, also frequently referred to as "as-a-service" models, are a relatively recent addition to the business landscape. That's not because they're complicated or advanced (though they are. From an operational perspective, it's much more complicated to own and service a product than just to sell it). It's because it wasn't until the widespread arrival of the Internet that they became viable.

Careful observers of outcome-based models will notice several variations. There are self-monitoring services, which replenish themselves automatically; subscription models, which charge a regular, generally time-based fee; and as-a-service businesses, which provide services specially tailored to your individual and dynamic needs.

Being a provider of outcome-based capabilities can increase your profits, improve your relationships with your customers, and increase customer loyalty. But like a platform business, they're not for everybody. Making the switch to an outcome-based model is a complex transformation best suited to companies with specific goals and capabilities.

OUTCOME-BASED MODEL 1: SELF-MONITORING PRODUCTS

"The moment of running out is a really bad moment for consumers,"[33] a spokesperson for Brita jabs in an ad promoting the company's automatically replenishing water filters. Brita is a great example of our first outcome-based model—self-monitoring products. Earlier in the book, we talked about Brita's Infinity Smart Water Pitcher, which uses embedded sensors to automatically order fresh filters through Amazon's Dash Replenishment system.

Working with Amazon Dash Replenishment, companies like Brita, Clorox, and others are providing automatic replenishments, service reminders, and other event-driven product-to-company scenarios. For busy customers, this is a godsend: no more trying to remember when you last replaced your Brita filter or whether you were supposed to pick one up at the store. The product not only monitors the situation but takes the next steps in ordering the part or service.

If self-service business models allow customers to interact with you on their own terms, then self-monitoring products are the next generation. They transcend the need for a customer to manage or even interact at all. And they assure that the product—whether that's a Brita filter or your car's oil filter—is always fresh, working, and usable.

Replacing human memory or involvement with sensor-based measurement and reordering is one of the biggest opportunities that the Internet of Things creates for brands and manufacturers. But companies that choose to adopt this model will also face some sticky decisions.

Let's say, for example, you're a washing-machine manufacturer, and you decide to add sensors into your product that automatically alert your company whenever the machine needs servicing. You, as the manufacturer, will automatically schedule and send an in-house repairperson to deal with any needed part replacements or machine failures. The customers, for their part, will automatically be charged for needed repairs. That's great news for you—you just picked up another source of revenue for your business. It's also great news for the customers—they don't have to guess about what's wrong with their washing machine or deal with unforeseen outages.

But it's not great news for the network of preferred distributors and repair people that used to install and service your washing machines. How do you decide who owns the customer relationship and ongoing revenue opportunity in these cases? How do you make a transition to this model over time?

Businesses that choose to make the switch should be aware that disruption, breaking traditions, reorganization, and structural changes will be a part of the fun.

OUTCOME-BASED MODEL 2: SUBSCRIBE-TO-THIS

Rent-the-Runway, a subscription business for fashion clothes; Pley, a subscription business for toys; Ditto, a subscription business for prescription eyewear. Each of these is an example of one of the hottest consumer business-model fads of the last few years: subscription.

Like any fad, the subscription craze is likely to birth a couple of winners, lots of losers, and a stream of great company names, but that's no reason to be discouraged by the subscription model—particularly given the unique opening that the Internet of Things is creating for subscription models by animating products and services with a digital heartbeat.

One of the clearest examples of this is usage-based insurance (UBI), which typically uses a proprietary plug-in device like the Progressive Snapshot or native software in the car to track your driving habits. Your monthly bill and risk evaluation are calculated by the volume and safety of your total driving. Ironically, usage-based insurance is really just converting one type of subscription business (uniform monthly car-insurance payments) into another (payments and risk based on how much you drive and the quality of that driving). It is estimated that by 2020, over fifty million US drivers will have tried usage-based insurance.[34]

This model will have a significant impact on driver behavior, of course, but its real impact might end up being to the insurance companies. Guess who might get into the car-insurance business? Perhaps automobile manufacturers? Companies using their product positions to extend services and other products will be a common and disruptive theme.

Zipcar, which provides on-demand car usage, is another form of outcome-based business model. The company blends a monthly subscription model with a per-use fee (either hourly or daily) to provide access to a variety of cars and trucks. Your subscription includes gas, insurance, and on-demand access to Zipcars at thousands of locations. None of it would be possible without the Internet of Things: customers are issued a credit card–sized smartcard with an embedded chip to unlock Zipcars they've reserved. RFID transponders on the windshield link with the card to identify the customer and remotely unlock the car. Mileage, usage, and location are tracked from the car, and a remote "kill" feature will turn the car off in case it's stolen. Each car is also equipped with significant operational and fleet-management capabilities to track maintenance and service status.[35]

B2B and established enterprises also have new opportunities to pursue subscription-based models. Many of the more complex, less obvious B2B subscription business models are using the Internet of Things to measure, provision, and manage their products or services and to improve experiences for their customers.

Kaeser Kompressoren is a hundred-year-old German air-compressor manufacturer that provides air-compression systems to manufacturing and chemical processing and other industrial companies. Recently, Kaeser has made the transition from selling cylinders of compressed air to selling, on a subscription basis, what its customers really want—reliable compressed air.

When Kaeser began installing sensors in their compressors, it found itself with a body of data that gave the company new insights into its customers' usage patterns and allowed it to improve its preventative maintenance. As Kaeser got smarter about customer use and how to avoid quality errors, it was able to make the transition to an "air-as-a-service" subscription program.

Through that program, Kaeser now guarantees both an uninterrupted supply of compressed air and full maintenance of the system. This also creates an interesting incentive swap: in its traditional business, making a service call actually generated revenue for Kaeser. Now that the company is a subscription business, it has become a cost. Kaeser has much more skin in the game to reduce necessary repairs.[36]

In the case of Kaeser and Zipcar, the customer is paying for use of specialized products without having to buy and own them, but the subscription model can also coexist with a product-purchase model.

Dropcam, for example, sells customers on an affordable home-surveillance camera and then provides optional recording and video storage services on a subscription basis. Likewise, Scout, another home-security business, sells a wide array of wireless, easy-to-install, and artfully designed sensors, monitors, and cameras that connect to a hub unit. Customers can choose to operate the hub as-is for security alarms, notifications, and recording. Or they can add a subscription to human-monitored surveillance services and on-site installation and response services. For both Dropcam and Scout, the real profit is in the subscription.

OUTCOME-BASED MODEL 3: AS-A-SERVICE

As-a-service is similar in some ways to the subscription and self-monitoring services models in that it replaces products that you used to own and operate with the usage and outcome of those products. But where, in a subscription, you more or less commit to a monthly amount, as-a-service charges for its services based on volume and quality. It also generally provides the ability to scale, both up and down, based on your particular needs.

The clearest example of this is Amazon Web Services, the industry's dominant cloud-computing provider and innovator. Although the technology of providing on-demand infrastructure and tools is a big part of the story, AWS's business model is its other significant innovation.

Traditionally, it was left to individual companies to build and operate data centers, procure large computer servers and network gear, and hire a staff to operate and monitor that data center. For obvious reasons, this was a less-than-ideal arrangement for smaller businesses. Then a new model emerged: rather than manage their own servers, businesses began renting data-center space from a provider. This was known as CoLo, or "colocation."

But even CoLo had its downsides. The software applications and database technology running on this infrastructure required a large up-front licensing fee and an annual maintenance fee—typically 15 to 20 percent of the original license fee. And again, you would have to hire specialized staff just to keep the applications running on the infrastructure.

Cloud computing turned this model on its head.

Instead of committing up front to buying computers or licenses, you now purchase just what you use. Rather than being responsible for operating and maintaining high availability and performance, your cloud provider (more likely than not, AWS) takes responsibility. Rather than being limited by inflexible and mostly underused capacity, you pay for a flexible amount based on your actual usage. Dramatically fewer employees are needed to manage this environment.

Another example of an Amazon as-a-service business is Fulfillment by Amazon (FBA), which sells access to Amazon's vast product-logistics and distribution network. Sellers have on-demand access to warehouses, goods transportation, and planning algorithms. How much should I purchase? How should I allocate it across the country? They can scale up and down as their business demands.

In the last few years, the as-a-service model has grown dramatically. Where it used to be primarily facilitated by cloud computing, the Internet of Things has hugely expanded the possible range of as-a-service businesses. IDC Manufacturing Insights estimates that 40 percent of top one hundred discrete manufacturers and 20 percent of Top 100 process manufacturers will provide product-as-service platforms by 2018.[37]

Rolls Royce now provides jet engines as a service for commercial airlines, moving the ownership of an airliner's engine and the responsibility for its care and maintenance back to Rolls Royce itself. Airlines pay a fee per engine flying hour to rent a Rolls Royce engine embedded with thousands of sensors. Those sensors stream information into Rolls Royce HQ, creating a digital twin of the engine that tracks real-time engine conditions and uses predictive analytics to plan for needed future maintenance. Airlines benefit from simplified operations, and Rolls Royce benefits from increased revenue (a 40 percent jump in 2015).[38]

Another benefit to businesses that use outcome-based models is a much tighter relationship with customers. At a B2B level, these businesses become more critical to management and operations and have much better data, making them valuable partners.

As companies move from a transaction-based business to a relationship- and services-based business, their value propositions become better aligned with their customers. Where vendors might previously have benefitted from required services or replacements, both vendors and their clients are incentivized to control costs, improve quality, and increase reliability.

Instead of pushing more product, vendors are aligned with customers on efficient operations and preventative maintenance. That reinforces the customer relationship, creating longer lifecycles and more strategic positioning.

NAVIGATING THE TRANSITION TO AN OUTCOME-BASED MODEL

In this chapter we've learned the outcome-based models and the results this approach can generate. But how do we get there?

Even in the easiest situation, making the switch to an outcome-based business is tricky. Shifting from a product or service company to offering "outcomes" will change almost everything about your organization.

In order to succeed, you'll need to offer significant differentiation from other offerings in your space and make significant internal changes to your team and company operations.

If you're considering whether to make the transition, here are a few things to keep in mind:

- *Channel Conflict.* As models change to outcomes-based services, manufacturers may provide services directly to their customers that have traditionally been provided by distributors. As a company, you'll need to handle this transition delicately to preserve customer relationships.
- *Customer Education.* Your customers will need to understand not only how your product and services are changing but any other implications the change might hold for them.
- *Accounting Uh-Ohs.* Investors love recurring-revenue business models, but the transition from nonrecurring revenue to recurring impacts many accounting treatments and often creates a revenue dip in the up-front periods. You'll need to communicate clearly with customers, investors, and others to help set their expectations.
- *Internal Reorganization.* As an outcome-based business, you will have contractual obligations to customers for specific service levels. In order to provide those and meet customer expectations, you'll need to restructure your company. Without changes to your operations, account management, and sales processes, you're unlikely to be able to provide proactive service that minimizes the number of issues you'll need to address.
- *New Talents.* The right people are key to making all of these transitions work. Specifically, product managers, partner managers, and business-model innovators are just as important as the technologists building connected products and services. There is always a shortage of architects and developers to fuel the technology-driven business cycle, but Amazon also hires more MBAs, by far, than any other technology company.[39]

Product management, partner management, and business-model inno-vation are all roles filled by great business talent. If you choose to adopt an outcome-based business model, it will be essential to understand that, while the technology is difficult, it's the nontechnical parts that will actu-ally make your business work. This is true for all business-model changes, including the next principle—making the IoT data the product.

Principle 8

The Data Is the Business Model

Nielsen, IRI, ListHub, Point2, IMS Health, and many more. There's a long list of data-broker companies that have built a thriving business by collecting, packaging, and reselling data. So far, though, it's difficult to find examples of IoT-based companies that have found success in packaging and selling IoT data.

Don't let that fool you.

The market potential for IoT data brokerage, or "data as a service," has yet to fully arrive, but it is looming thanks to the confluence of sensors, cloud computing, third-party data sources, and APIs. Like the rest of the IoT market, it will be big. Gartner predicts that "10% of organizations will have a highly profitable business unit specifically for productizing and commercializing their information assets."[40]

Principle 8: Through the Internet of Things, companies can collect an unprecedented volume and variety of data—the new "black gold"—which they will syndicate to create valuable new businesses and revenue streams.

In this chapter we will explore how the data you own is an essential element in any IoT strategy and how to walk the delicate line between monetization and protecting individual privacy.

Already we're seeing smart-home companies selling IoT-generated data to advertisers or insurance companies, cargo ship transit and port arrival information being sold to financial trading companies, and building and appliance energy-consumption data being sold to utility companies. It's a sophisticated business and a growing opportunity for companies in the midst of building and leveraging their IoT strategies. To get there, you'll need to build your data assets strategically and offer others the ability to access these assets simply.

If you're part of a company that's even remotely interested in building a revenue stream around IoT data, now is the time to start planning. Setting yourself up to collect data through your products and services today will give you the assets you need to attack the IoT data market soon in the future.

Amazon—which, as already noted, is already using the Internet of Things to improve customer experiences, drive operational improvements, and build new business models (the IoT triple threat)—is so far holding off on announcing any serious IoT-data-broker plays.

That might seem strange in the face of their move-fast-and-break-things approach to other new markets. With drones, machine learning, and voice recognition, Bezos has played for the first-mover advantage, but a data business is ruled by different dynamics. There's not much to be gained—and, frankly, a lot to lose—by jumping in before there are enough customers to support your business.

While the company bides its time, Amazon is likely to carry on collecting as much data as possible. When the right time does come, Amazon wants to be prepared to dive in. Or, if for some reason, Amazon decides it's not strategic after all, the company will still be set up to use its data as it always has—to drive consumer experience through personal recommendations, personalization, and data-based advertising models.

THE SYNDICATION BUSINESS MODEL

Once you feel the time is right to dive into the data market, you'll need a business model. The most popular approach to data sales is through syndication, the act of collecting, packaging, and selling access to data. Or, as the Harvard Business Review described it,

> Syndication involves the sale of the same good to many customers, who then integrate it with other offerings and redistribute it...syndication is a radically different way of structuring business than anything that's come before. It requires entrepreneurs and executives to rethink their strategies and reshape their organizations, to change the way they interact with customers and partner with other entities, and to pioneer new models for collecting revenues and earning profits. Those that best understand the dynamics of syndication—that are able to position themselves in the most lucrative nodes of syndication networks—will be the ones that thrive in the Internet era.[41]

Data brokers like Experian, Nielsen, and Dun & Bradstreet have all worn a firm path here, building large, successful businesses on some variation of the syndication model.

Over the years, the old-school syndication models they used have been upgraded by digital capabilities, progressing from distributing paper reports and CD-ROM-based data sets to APIs, which allow for the real-time integration of data and critical business systems.

Some IoT-based companies will use data syndication as their primary business model. For others, it will be just one of many revenue streams.

One early entrant to the IoT data sales industry is Inrix, a company based in Kirkland, Washington. Inrix's core business is selling real-time traffic and automotive data to car manufacturers like Tesla and BMW. You can think of their business in two major chunks—sourcing the data and then selling the data.

On the sourcing side, they collect data from many places—cell phones, sensors in cars, commercial fleets, fleet management software companies, chipset manufacturers, public data sources such as roads with coiled sensors in them, and roadside RFID sensors.

Inrix then munges the data, combining and integrating disparate data streams to meet specific customer needs. Their primary business is in selling real-time traffic data to car manufacturers, which use the data to power their navigation systems. This data has a very short half-life—information about the amount of traffic on a road is really only valuable at the time that that traffic exists. Its value decays quickly.

Inrix also provides a range-prediction tool for electric vehicles, which uses algorithms to calculate a vehicle's range on a given electric charge based on weather, road, and traffic conditions. It provides intermodal transportation data to power wayfinding calculations about driving, walking, and for public transportation. It even sells historical traffic information to public and infrastructure-planning companies that need detailed traffic-pattern data.

All of Inrix's data is sourced from and accessed via APIs. Some of the companies Inrix sources data from are also data-as-a-service IoT-based businesses, such as chipset manufacturers and digital-map-data providers, primarily HERE and Tele Atlas.

In each of these cases, it has taken years of focus and investment to build and develop a data-brokering business model. This is important if you're thinking about integrating data brokering or data syndication into your business. For companies not already in this space, creating this kind of long-term focus and patience will be the largest hurdle to breaking in.

In addition to direct syndication, there are also other indirect business models for working with data.

Some companies, like Google, use data to drive advertising. Google has collected immense amounts of information about the search habits and use cases of its customers. It won't sell you that data directly, but it will sell you the insights that they've gleaned from it in the form of targeted, direct advertising.

Through Nest, a Google subsidiary, Google also sells insights about customers' energy, appliance, and utility use to utility companies. The revenue potential of even this submarket is estimated in the hundreds of millions per year.[42]

DATA-AS-A-SERVICE VIA APIS

If you're thinking about building out a data market of your own, one of the most important decisions you'll make is about how to distribute that information to others so that they can derive the most possible value from the data you've collected.

In nearly all cases, there's really only one right approach here—using an API to allow technology developers to easily leverage your services and capabilities in real time.

Sometimes it's the volume or veracity of your data that will make it valuable—a huge set of data about a customer's search habits, for example, is likely more useful than just the last hour of that person's search history. But oftentimes, as in the case of Inrix's traffic data, it's the real-time nature that will make your data most valuable to your customers. It's the ability to see what is happening right *now* at any given time.

APIs allow you to incorporate data bought from someone else into your technology applications in real time. APIs are also a more operationally efficient way to share data. There are still a lot of data companies that distribute data via CD, for example. But with an API, you won't need to add extra infrastructure or significantly more headcount to scale and distribute that data to more and more customers.

There are literally thousands of APIs that developers can access to leverage the capabilities of others. Sometimes the capability behind an API is some form of infrastructure, like cloud computing. Sometimes that capability is a transaction—companies can use APIs to manage their UPS shipments, for example. Sometimes it even integrates two or more products together. APIs are the infrastructural backbone that allows Amazon's Alexa and Ford cars to send updates to one another.

One of the most interesting and robust categories you'll find in IoT-enabled APIs is in weather data. That's due mostly to the huge number of probes, buoys, gauges, and other instruments that have been deployed around the world to source real-time weather data. Those sensors act as the backbone for a growing group of companies providing data-as-a-service weather APIs.

Zappos, for example, uses a weather-based data-as-a-service API to deliver personalized weather-aware marketing and customer engagement ads and content. If it senses there's a pattern of rain in your area, it might serve you an ad for rain boots.

"We want to make sure if it's gonna rain in your neighborhood, how can we stay personal with you and show you something that's relevant for you," explained Lisa Archambault, Zappos's head of demand generation, at a 2014 conference.[43]

PRIVACY, OWNERSHIP, AND SECURITY: NAVIGATING THE WILD WEST OF DATA

The biggest risk—and the biggest opportunity—of the IoT data-brokerage business is its lack of regulation on privacy, data ownership, and security. We can start to get a sense of why this is by putting ourselves in the mind-set of a farmer.

As a farmer, there are plenty of things you'll need to worry about—the prices of commodity products, the price of fuel, how to take care of your employees, the weather, how to sustain soil health, and safety are all on the list. That's why companies like Climate Corporation have combed so much of American farmland for data and offer services help farmers track and maintain soil health.

But at the top of that list is a concern about who owns and profits from the data on your farm, crops, and productivity. According to a 2016 American Farm Bureau Federation survey,[44] 77 percent of respondents are "concerned about which entities can access their farm data, and whether it could be used for regulatory purposes."[45]

The lack of stable and well-understood regulation around data ownership, control, and monetization make data syndication a kind of wild, wild West.

With the fast-growing number of endpoint devices and IoT's networked nature, securing the Internet of Things is perhaps the biggest threat to the promise of connected devices. Privacy, or the rights of individuals to understand, agree, or opt out of data collected about them, is another big one.

In the industrial and B2B IoT market, there are very few protocols and norms for negotiating and licensing data ownership. Individual deals often determine any rules and regulations between two companies around data processing and access. What few regulations there are can vary by geography and are dynamic.

The consumer segment, where data is collected from users of apps and products, is even more complex. Privacy and making consumer control transparent and easy-to-manage approaches are becoming a multi-front battle. This includes public policy and laws that are not advancing at the speed of technology and product capabilities. Autonomous cars are an example of where policy and laws are behind where the reality of the market is at.

Even the separation between the B2B and consumer markets is artificial and blurred. Data collected in employment situations is often subject to different interpretations and obligations. Who owns the data? Who profits from the data? Where do company priorities collide with individual rights and choices?

For example, if a construction company sells an insurance company data about workplace accidents and the physical well-being of its workers, could that insurance company use that information to approve or deny an individual's health insurance application? How should that information be managed relative to the individual's health and privacy rules?

■ ■ ■

LEGAL LANDSCAPE FOR PRIVACY—IT'S GETTING MORE COMPLEX

For companies in the data space, managing and protecting data privacy will be opaque, risky, and hard to evaluate. The very definition of privacy is situational, varying by country, industry, and context. It is also extremely personal, with significant volumes of private customer information at stake.

Getting privacy right will win you customers; getting it wrong could be a major blow to your business. In both consumer and industrial IoT businesses, it will be essential to create the processes and architecture up front that allow you to manage data privacy and react to evolving business and regulatory requirements and standards.

It's helpful to think about privacy as a three-legged stool. The first leg of the stool is your privacy policy itself, shaped by legal and international policy inputs. The second is the impact of privacy on your business model and value proposition. The third leg of the stool is your internal process and architecture for managing and adapting your privacy strategy. Security is a complementary but separate topic.

From the business-model standpoint, privacy can be both a key design constraint and important aspect of flexibility. On one hand, data linked to individuals can be important to the features and capabilities of IoT-enabled business models, even in industrial cases. Think about IoT devices that track individual location and activity levels; facial, speech, or other security identification devices and capabilities; or authentication devices managing access to resources. On the other, companies may have their own reasons for using discretion in managing, transmitting, and retaining location data.

The third leg of the stool is made up of the processes needed to manage privacy, typically tied to data access and management processes, processes required to manage the commitments made in the privacy policies they commit to, and capabilities to report and prove compliance with legal obligations.

I have a client that is a legacy software company transitioning to an API-driven platform model. As we were developing the platform business strategy and impact to architecture, we discovered that geography-aware capabilities could be a clear differentiator for both the users of the solution, as well as for my client's company. With geo-aware capabilities, users are able to specify business rules regarding the location and tracking of content to keep it within certain jurisdictions.

The de facto interpretation and approach to a company's legal compliance accountabilities for privacy was that they were accountable to the jurisdiction in which the data was stored, not where users were located.

At the time, US companies were able to comply with all EU-country laws by self-certifying compliance with the Safe Harbor Privacy Principles.[46]

> *Notice.* Individuals must be informed that their data is being collected and about how it will be used.
>
> *Choice.* Individuals must have the option to opt out of the collection and forward transfer of the data to third parties.
>
> *Onward Transfer.* Transfers of data to third parties may only occur to other organizations that follow adequate data-protection principles.
>
> *Security.* Reasonable efforts must be made to prevent loss of collected information.
>
> *Data Integrity.* Data must be relevant and reliable for the purpose it was collected for.
>
> *Access.* Individuals must be able to access information held about them and correct or delete it if it is inaccurate.
>
> *Enforcement.* There must be effective means of enforcing these rules.

This allowed US-based companies two critical operational benefits—first, they could transfer data to the United States without architecting geo-aware services. Secondly, they could easily comply with each EU country's laws through one self-certification.

That was until Max Schrems came along. Schrems, an Austrian law student, decided to take on Facebook in a David versus Goliath legal battle after Snowden revealed that US agencies were reviewing European data that passed through US data centers. His goal was to prevent US companies from transporting EU citizens' data outside the European Union.

Schrems's lawsuit was successful, effectively invalidating Safe Harbor. Individual European countries can suspend data transfers if they (not the European Union) rule them a violation of individual privacy.

The implications of this to consumer and industrial IoT services are deep and dynamic. As *Fortune*'s David Meyer commented, "This isn't just about Facebook—it could be very bad news for many U.S. multinationals with a European presence."[47]

For all companies in the data space, including your legal partner(s) as an integral part of the team is key. The stakes get higher if you're planning to deploy to the European Union. But since security compliance can have a major impact on architecture design, I'd recommend all companies keep security at the forefront of their approach in early prototypes and pilots.

KEY QUESTIONS TO ADDRESS IN DEVELOPMENT OF PRIVACY STRATEGIES FOR IOT

1. What data and events will be collected that either independently or, when merged with others, can identify an individual?
2. Will this data be transferred and stored beyond the device to a central server or cloud storage?
3. Will the IoT devices and service be designed to operate internationally?
4. What geography and access-management capabilities are required, and how might these provide competitive differentiation?
5. What broader approaches should you be taking to protect your business from the downsides of any future regulations?

■ ■ ■

For companies considering the data-broker business, it will be essential to be both proactive and transparent about how you manage and regulate data.

The downside of twenty-six billion endpoints by 2020 is that there are twenty-six billion endpoints to secure, keep current, manage the operations of, and understand when illicit activity or breaches have happened. The security and operational management of IoT devices are both a major design and ongoing operational and security challenge. Building your security framework and requirements for prevention, detection, and recovery from the start is often referred to as "security by design."

From the start, you should call on both internal and external legal help to develop your IoT strategy. This approach is known as "legal by design." Like the more popular "security by design," legal by design means recognizing the role that legal and security concerns play in the entire product-design life cycle. They cannot be separated or considered just as afterthoughts in the design process.

Specific requirements and quickly changing privacy obligations can be a risk to entering the market. But if you get out ahead of developing norms and legal standards from the start, that uncertainty and complexity can actually become a strategic advantage.

DEPLOYING AN IOT-DRIVEN DATA-BROKER BUSINESS

Hopefully you now see the huge possible upside of an IoT-driven data-broker business. You're ready to dive in. What will you need to develop this asset? How should you move ahead?

First, you need to get clear on your strategy. What kinds of data assets could you best create through your business? What markets and clients would find this data valuable? What other contextual data could you bring in to enrich it and make it even more valuable? What might be your licensing or subscription approach? What possible legal or other conflicts might keep you from pursuing this opportunity? The first step of developing an IoT-driven data-broker business is to move from an opaque, high-level view of what your business could be to specific, real examples to bring clarity and definition.

Second, based on the strategy and use cases you decide to pursue, you'll need to understand exactly how to make the data you collect as valuable as possible. What kind of processing would you need to do to on the raw data before you could sell it to others? What kind of parameters should you set around data collection? For your own use, you might only plan on collecting a subset of location, movement, or use data from your sensors, but, given the declining cost of collecting and storing data, it might be smart to collect more than you'd ever think you need. Sometime in the future, the fact that you've collected that data might create new opportunities and uses. Imagine you had a bunch of buoys out in the ocean. For personal purposes, you might only need to know if the water moves above or below certain temperatures, but you might find upon reflection that some portion of the market actually values the real-time temperature of the water. In that case, you'd need to make a quick pivot to collect the temperature of the water every fifteen seconds.

Third, you'll need to build a background in the information-brokering business and a keen understanding of potential clients for your data. You'll need to understand how to optimize value for these clients and develop actual go-to-market skills. How will you package this data? How will you approach the market? How will you develop new clients and service existing clients once you have them? In the case of the buoy company, for example, this might mean building out a marketing or sales team that understands how to approach the institutions and broader market that would be interested.

Fourth, you'll need to install leadership focused on curating data as intellectual property (IP). Most organizations understand and value IP but don't understand the value of data. Just as you value other kinds of IP in your business, you'll need to develop expertise in managing data as a commercial asset.

Doug Hubbard is a consultant focused on applied-information economics. As he has explains, innovation teams that include the CIO or other IT leaders can "take raw information and turn it into a product...you need the equivalent of an actuary in IT."[48] Design, technology, and brand are all examples of IP curated and valued by organizations. Data needs to be one of them. In so doing, you'll naturally find ways to make that data more valuable.

And finally, you'll need to determine pricing and licensing approaches. As with so many assets and values, the beauty of data is in the eye of the beholder. Determining the value of your product and how to price a potential data asset will take triangulation and experience, but there are a few steps to get you off on the right track.

1. *Figure Out the Replacement Cost.* If someone had to go build the data set, what would it take in terms of cost, time, and distraction?
2. *Understand How the Data Might Be Used.* If possible, do a "with the data" financial analysis and a "without the data" financial analysis.
3. *Benchmark.* Compare your data asset to others, and understand both their pricing and the value of the data.

These steps might seem unnecessary in a market that's still young, but by diving in early, focusing on defining your product, and understanding the market and its value, you'll be setting your company up to pounce on a huge opportunity.

There will be many entrants into the IoT data-syndication business. Only a few will find success. And, as with many things in business, timing will be everything.

Principle 9

Disrupting the Industry-
Value Chain

*Our industry does not respect tradition. It only respects
innovation.*

—Satya Nadella, Microsoft CEO

When I worked at Amazon from early 2002 through late 2005, it was a relatively simple company. There were roughly three thousand employees at corporate headquarters (not including customer service and fulfillment associates). Almost all of our annual revenue, which at the time clocked in at just below $4 billion, came from retail sales in three categories—books, music, and video retail (primarily DVDs at that point). There were just five Amazon fulfillment centers in North America.

The holiday season of 2002 was an almost $1.5 billion-revenue quarter. Scaling was critical in every part of the business, and this was the first holiday season that Amazon's corporate staff didn't spend the holidays working in fulfillment centers to help out on order surge during the busiest weeks of the year.

Just look at it today. In 2016, revenue was estimated at $134 billion.[49] There are approximately one hundred North American fulfillment centers (three hundred worldwide) and still adding. And no longer is Amazon just an e-commerce retailer. Today, it's a conglomerate business that spans all manner of consumer products, marketplaces, cloud technology, and B2B tools and services.

But here's what most people don't realize: Amazon uses a simple formula to enable this kind of growth. And once you understand what it is, it's easy to integrate into your own thinking about growth and strategic planning.

Principle 9: Innovation and growth come from a constant exploration and strategic bets into new products and services. The Amazon way to identify those products and services is typically to start with your existing product and services and move up and down the value chain. The Internet of Things creates new opportunities for expansion up and down the value chain.

In previous chapters we've learned how Amazon builds platforms focused on measuring outcomes and leveraging data to build one of the most valuable companies in the world. In this chapter we see how Amazon has gone up and down the value chain to identify places where providing services to itself would create cost savings, give the company more control, and create exciting new business opportunities. IoT is becoming a key enabler of building innovative capabilities along different value chains and altering the traditions of how business has been done.

A value chain is the end-to-end set of processes and activities for an industry. When Amazon first started, it was focused on being a first-generation e-commerce retailer. They quickly allowed others to sell used items, books, and compact discs on the same item page as new inventory. Then they moved to allowing third-party sellers to create new items to sell at Amazon and allowing multiple sellers of the same item through the Marketplace platform. From there, Amazon expanded rapidly into new retail categories including apparel, sporting goods, and even musical instruments. Amazon then began creating proprietary brands of products. Amazon enables third-party sellers to effectively outsource logistics and delivery capabilities to Amazon. The list goes on and on.

The most recent iteration of Amazon's value-chain expansion is into the transportation industry. Recently, the company has begun leasing its own jets to transport its retail inventory more cost effectively and with more control. Analysts have estimated that this will save the company upward of $400 million a year.[50]

HOW AMAZON EXPANDS INTO NEW BUSINESSES

In his 2014 shareholder letter, Bezos outlined three Amazon businesses now operating at scale.

> To our shareowners:
>
> A dreamy business offering has at least four characteristics. Customers love it, it can grow to very large size, it has strong returns on capital, and it's durable in time—with the potential to endure for decades. When you find one of these, don't just swipe right, get married.
>
> Well, I'm pleased to report that Amazon hasn't been monogamous in this regard. After two decades of risk taking and teamwork, and with generous helpings of good fortune all along the way, we are now happily wed to what I believe are three such life partners: Marketplace, Prime, and AWS. Each of these offerings was a bold bet at first, and sensible people worried (often!) that they could not work. But at this point, it's become pretty clear how special they are and how lucky we are to have them. It's also clear that there are no sinecures in business. We know it's our job to always nourish and fortify them.
>
> We'll approach the job with our usual tools: customer obsession rather than competitor focus, heartfelt passion for invention, commitment to operational excellence, and a willingness to think

long-term. With good execution and a bit of continuing good luck, Marketplace, Prime, and AWS can be serving customers and earning financial returns for many years to come.[51]

Amazon's business is even broader than these three "dreamy" businesses. They've expanded far beyond into a wide range of types of businesses, both up and down different industry value chains.

The formation of AWS, the market leader in cloud technology, started out as a simple move to improve technical efficiency. When I was at Amazon, each team owned, engineered, and operated its own computing infrastructure. What became apparent was that we were not taking advantage of economies of scale: custom configurations and nonstandardized hardware led to more expensive servers; infrastructure sat idle a large portion of the time (with no load sharing, infrastructure had to be designed for peak use); and each team developed its own operating and support approach.

So, eventually, we decided to separate out computing infrastructure into a central function. This was an important start, but the separation itself wasn't going to make our technology infrastructure world class.

Always the rationalist, Bezos would say something wise like, "You know, this split may be a good idea, but it's only by having external customers that we'll have the feedback and expectations to turn this into something world class. So what we're going to do is to turn this around and expose it to external developers, because that's what's going to make the infrastructure good enough for our internal teams."

It didn't take long for Amazon to see that external developers loved this service and that it could be a great business. AWS was born, and the rest is history.

Through this kind of search for operational efficiencies, Amazon has expanded into a wide range of conglomerate businesses, building new tools and services that both its own internal teams and outside customers can use. At Amazon, the breadth of this conglomerate business includes the following:

Acquisitions. Over sixty-four acquisitions, including Kiva Systems, a warehouse robotics company; Zappos, an online footwear company; and Annapurna Labs, a system-on-a-chip microelectronics company selling to hardware OEMs.

Private-Label Brands. Amazon designs, markets, and manufactures or contracts for manufacturer many consumer brands currently for sale at Amazon.com, including apparel brands such as Lark & Ro and North Eleven, outdoor-furniture brand Strathwood, electronics brand AmazonBasics, and Prime Pantry, a consumables brand.

Website Brands. Amazon also owns and operates many other websites, including IMDB.com, Woot.com, Zappos.com, Diapers.com, Fabric. com, Twitch.tv, dbreview.com, Endless.com, and of course Createspace. com, where I created this book.

Products and Services. The number makes them hard to tally, but beyond retail services, Amazon sells all of the following, if not more, as independent capabilities:

- Order fulfillment services—Fulfillment By Amazon (FBA) allows sellers to warehouse and fulfill orders from Amazon fulfillment centers.
- Payments processing—Payments by Amazon is used by retailers as a trusted payment gateway.
- AWS S2 (simple storage) and EC2 (elastic cloud compute)—these are two of the many AWS cloud-computing products.
- Amazon Fire Stick—this is a proprietary device used by customers in their TVs to access Amazon and many other content providers, like ESPN.
- System on a Chip Design—Annapurna Labs is a company that designs and sells specially designed computer chips used in networking devices.
- Amazon Publishing—this is a full-service publishing arm of Amazon, cultivating authors and books.

- Advertising services—this service allows sellers to bid for product-placement ads at Amazon.
- Twitch—this is a live video service and social platform enabling customers to watch events, primarily e-sport events.

There are also several major internal capabilities Amazon has today that it could one day decide to offer to other companies. They could one day become Amazon businesses.

- *Electronic Device (Phone/Tablet) Design.* Could Amazon figure out a way to democratize device design and manufacturing by removing obstacles and gatekeepers, perhaps similar to how CreateSpace has opened up book publishing and distribution?
- *Content Production, Including TV Shows and Games.* This area has a strong potential for creating a platform business by removing the barriers and complexities of original-content production and distribution. This could be a huge win for both Amazon and people who want to tell stories via video or game production.
- *Robots Used in Warehouses.* Kiva was an acquisition and had external customers. For competitive reasons, Amazon has made this a proprietary and internal capability only. Will they open it back out to others at some point?
- *Photography Studios and Image Services.* Driven in particular by the apparel category, Amazon has developed scalable processes for creating and managing images. This would be a valuable "as-a-service" capability for other brands to leverage.

There are major new businesses and capabilities are being hatched right now. Amazon's proprietary air logistics capability, *Prime Air*, will deliver Amazon cost savings and control for parcel logistics. Amazon shipping is focused on international product-sourcing logistics, like ocean-going freight. Amazon Business Supplies is selling business products and supplies, and Amazon's machine learning makes it easy, in relative terms, for any developer to include machine-learning capabilities in their products.

These are the big bets that might become the "dreamy business offerings" touted by Bezos in shareholder letters of the next five to ten years.

THE IOT SUPPLY-CHAIN ADVANTAGE

As we've explained throughout this book, there are many different ways that Amazon is using IoT to build new integration and new scenarios across the value chain. They're building Echo as a completely new voice-driven interface for customers, but they're also using Alexa as a platform for others to leverage that ability.

As it did in Amazon's case, IoT can help you integrate across the value chain—particularly in areas where it was very difficult to create before.

Let's look at a non-Amazon example. If you manage commercial buildings, you're also running an HVAC system to control temperature and air quality. As the operator running that system, you have two maintenance choices: you either wait for something to go wrong, or you do an inspection to understand how it's operating and what service needs it might have. By adding connected sensors to the equation, though, you could get real-time information allowing the prediction of maintenance issues, understanding how the HVAC is operating, and optimizing runtime operations in real time. If you were the company or brand that actually built that HVAC, installing IoT sensors sets you up to not only sell those systems but to take responsibility for their maintenance in an as-a-service model.

German engineering firm Thyssen-Krup has done the same thing with elevators, connecting them to the cloud with Microsoft's Azure IoT services to monitor everything from motor temperature to shaft alignment, cab speed, and door functioning. The company combines this data into a dashboard alerting technicians about immediate maintenance needs, allowing the technicians to instantly diagnose problems.

There are plenty of other possibilities too. Imagine you're shipping temperature-sensitive material from overseas. That material needs to maintain a tight chain of custody—in other words, you need to know where it is and what temperature state it's in at all times. Traditionally, these types of situations have relied on manual inspections that collect a few key data points to fill you in on the condition the material is in and whether there have been any intrusions. (Theft, change of temperature, etc.) With connected sensors, though, you could create a much tighter custody of that service chain. If the supplier of that temperature-sensitive equipment developed its own specialized IoT tracking of those products, the supplier could then turn around and sell that to other companies transporting sensitive materials.

IDENTIFYING OPPORTUNITIES ACROSS THE VALUE CHAIN

How can you follow Amazon's lead in building a conglomerate set of businesses and capabilities utilizing a value-chain mentality? What can you learn from Amazon's strategy or planning to continue a growth rate that, at Amazon's size, is incredibly hard? How does Amazon plan to become not just the biggest retailer on earth but perhaps the biggest company? And what role does IoT play in this?

There are no simple answers, of course, but you can set yourself on the right course by adopting a belief held by Bezos: "Your margin is my opportunity."[52] If you can create a better, lower-cost, more flexible self-service way to do what another company is doing, that's a good candidate for a space to enter as a competitor.

To create a business culture modeled after Amazon's dogged pursuit of innovation, I suggest doing as Amazon does—entering an industry at one point in the value chain, looking upstream, looking downstream, and then asking five fundamental questions.

- First, where is there a broken customer experience? Lack of integration, lack of price and availability transparency, and arcane business practices are signs of a broken customer experience.

- Second, what services or technologies are your company paying for today that you could build and operate yourself to make your business more profitable?
- Third, how do you build those services and products well enough that other outside parties can also use them?
- Fourth, where do these conditions exist where there are attractive margins?
- And finally, how would IoT either fix that broken customer experience, help you deliver services or technologies at a lower cost to yourself and others, or allow you to create a different value proposition for your target customer?

There are formal ways of understanding an industry in this manner. *Harvard Business Review*'s classic "How to Map Your Industry's Profit Pool"[53] outlines the process of mapping your industry's value chain, including revenue and margin percentage at each step of the way. The summary is as follows:

1. Define the industry and value chain. Create boundaries and a definition of the industry you are evaluating.
2. Define the size of the revenue and profit pool. For each major step in the value chain, estimate the size of revenue and profits or margin percentages.
3. Create a visualization. This is typically accomplished by lining up the industry value chain from left to right and creating a bar graph for each step of the value chain. Assume the Y axis is "margin percentage" and the X axis is "revenue size."

At Amazon, we called this the "launch and learn strategy." You're entering an industry from one business point and then learning the industry to identify new opportunities. Sitting down and walking through this value-chain analysis allows for understanding and evaluation of your business options.

Doing this industry value-chain analysis is just the start. Then you'll need to sit down with your team and ask them some deeper, more disruptive, customer-obsessed and IoT-related questions. Below are the questions that I often ask myself to identify competitive and business-model opportunities in new industries.

- Who are the gatekeepers and regulators, and what are the regulations that preserve the status quo? How do they create barriers to entry and change? What if these gatekeepers and regulations did not exist or were circumvented?
- Who are the middlemen and brokers? What "value add" do they provide? How could this value be unlocked through data, integration, transparency, and accessibility?
- What is the true value delivered to a customer? Building from the HVAC situation, do the customers buy air conditioners, or do they really want value-efficient and comfortable building environments?
- Are selection and demand disaggregated? If transparency to selection, availability, pricing, product data, and performance were provided, what would change?
- What is the current provisioning, operating, and payment model? If these could be changed, be transformed to "as-a-service" or to a group/crowd ownership model, how would the business be changed? This is the question that really makes cloud computing such a hit—it switches technology capabilities from "taking a long time" to "on demand" and switches companies from "paid up front" to "pay by use."
- What operating data, if provided in real time, would help your customers be smarter about using your products and services (or other products and services in the value chain)? How could you provide all or parts of this data?
- What are the capital intensive aspects of the value chain? Could use of those capital intensive assets be improved? What data

and bottlenecks would need to be changed? Figuring out how to more efficiently use capital assets is the fundamental value behind many new business models.

- What suboptimized performance such as quality, maintenance, utilization, failures, or bottlenecks could be improved with key events or "math equations"? What algorithms could improve these performance factors?
- What are the broad operating risks of the industry? What early-warning and operating data would highlight or mitigate these risks? What sensors could provide early insights and data into these risks?
- What real-time adjustments could be made to improve key performance points? What data would be required to drive that adjustment? What type of actuator or control adjustment would be needed to make this adjustment? For example, GE is coordinating wind turbines to make real-time adjustments to optimize energy production based on the wind conditions.
- How could interactions between parties in the value chain be made "self-service" and integrated in nature and be changed to "on demand"? How would we eliminate all needs to talk to another person and make the situation so obvious, predictive, and real time in nature that lag between "customer need" and "need fulfilled" approaches zero?
- How do you make your capability truly "self-service" for purchasing, initialization, and operations? This is a baseline rule for a capability at Amazon.
- What is unnecessarily complex in the value chain (or constraint that is a long-held belief or approach)? What assumption or approach would need to change to improve?
- How does each "customer" in the value chain try to gain leverage, negotiate, or try to circumvent (go direct) with its supplier?
- How would each customer in the value chain finish the statement "Your product/service sucks because..."? You could ask the more

politically correct question, such as "What is the customer pain-point?" but that's not how Amazon would ask the question. An operator asks, "Why did we fail our customer; why did we have this issue?" Being self-critical and having the beginner's mind-set are a valuable mentality in trying to innovate and improve.

- What information and process steps are not integrated between systems and organizations? What would be the benefit of seamless data and process integration across the value chain?
- What data would make a difference to my customers or to operating my business more effectively? How could sensors collect this data? This is the fundamental open-ended question that IoT enables.

If you carefully consider each of these questions, with a bias toward challenging the status quo and starting with the customer, you'll be well on your way to identifying some of the top opportunities in your industry for moving up and down your value chain.

Principle 10

Synergies of the Flywheel

The volume and variety of Amazon's retail business are the stuff of legends, but the Amazon retail business is all centered on a rather simple concept—the flywheel. Consider the physics behind a flywheel: a rotating mechanical device that builds and stores more and more energy the more it rotates. In a business, there are certain forces that generate momentum. Thinking about your business as a flywheel—determining what factors will generate and sustain the most momentum in creating growth—will help you identify the most important levers of your business.

Bezos may have borrowed the flywheel concept from strategy guru Jim Collins, author of *Good to Great*. In addition to a powerful business strategy, the flywheel idea is a useful tool for communicating the company's sometimes puzzling decisions to employees and outsiders.

Principle 10: If you have a clear understanding of the systems dynamics—or flywheel model—of your business, you can use the Internet of Things to identify and execute on opportunities and risks in your business.

In this chapter, we'll talk about how to build a flywheel for your Internet of Things strategy. Once you've worked through some of your early questions on IoT strategy and have a stronger sense of what your moves should be, this will help you tie them together strategically so that your business decisions are mutually reinforcing and beneficial.

John Rossman

I started at Amazon in early 2002 with the mission of dramatically impacting a major part of that flywheel—adding thousands of sellers, who would add millions of items to Amazon's selection.

Up to that point, the flywheel had been limited in momentum. Essentially all selection was in three categories—books, music and video—and almost all of those products were being purchased and resold by Amazon, with limited third-party sellers participating.

Amazon, for its part, had already tried to launch a third-party seller program twice. Both attempts were unsuccessful. Bezos writes, "Marketplace's early days were not easy. First, we launched Amazon Auctions. I think seven people came, if you count my parents and siblings. Auctions transformed into zShops, which was basically a fixed price version of Auctions. Again, no customers."[54]

There are likely several reasons why these early versions failed, but certainly high on that list is because Amazon hadn't made things easy or simple enough for either set of customers they were trying to attract. Tools for the seller (customer 1) were limiting and hard to use, and the consumer experience (customer 2) had a poor discovery and shopping experience and was forced to checkout and pay separately for third-party products.

A big part of my job as the director of merchant integration was to add to the first Amazon leadership principle of customer obsession and to bring seller obsession to the business. We knew that we had to make great tools and a great business for sellers if we wanted to create the virtuous cycle we had pictured.

How did we do that? Here's Bezos again:

Internally, Marketplace was known as SDP for Single Detail Page. The idea was to take our most valuable retail real estate—our product detail pages—and let third-party sellers compete against our own retail category managers. It was more convenient for customers, and within a year, it accounted for 5% of units. Today, more than 40% of our units are sold by more than two million third-party sellers worldwide. Customers ordered more than two billion units from sellers in 2014.

The success of this hybrid model accelerated the Amazon flywheel. Customers were initially drawn by our fast-growing selection of Amazon-sold products at great prices with a great customer experience. By then allowing third parties to offer products side-by-side, we became more attractive to customers, which drew even more sellers. This also added to our economies of scale, which we passed along by lowering prices and eliminating shipping fees for qualifying orders.

Having introduced these programs in the U.S., we rolled them out as quickly as we could to our other geographies. The result was a marketplace that became seamlessly integrated with all of our global websites.[55]

First, let's revisit how Amazon thinks about and uses the flywheel.

THE FLYWHEEL

The Amazon Flywheel is a long-tested systems-dynamic view of Amazon's core retail and Marketplace businesses.

The original flywheel looks simple, but in reality it's quite nuanced. Lower prices and a great customer experience will bring customers in, Bezos reasoned. High traffic will lead to higher sales numbers, which draw in more third-party commission-paying sellers. Each additional seller allows Amazon to get more out of fixed costs like fulfillment centers and the servers needed to run the website. This greater efficiency then enables it to lower prices further. More sellers also leads to better selection, which all comes full circle back to a better customer experience.

As author and former Amazon executive Brad Stone writes in *The Everything Store*,

> Bezos and his lieutenants sketched their own virtuous cycle, which they believed powered their business. It went something like this: lower prices led to more customer visits. More customers increased the volume of sales and attracted more commission-paying third-party sellers to the site. That allowed Amazon to get more out of fixed costs like the fulfillment centers and the servers needed to run the website. This greater efficiency then enabled it to lower prices further. Feed any part of this flywheel, they reasoned, and it should accelerate the loop.[56]

While I was at Amazon, we used the flywheel to develop, rationalize, and coordinate important investments and understand how companies, which on one hand might be viewed as competitors, could actually be leveraged as important partners to accomplish long-term goals. A flywheel can help you see nonobvious opportunities and prioritize partners and clients. Bezos has often said, "We are willing to be misunderstood for long periods of time."[57] These areas of being "misunderstood" are often key leverage points in Amazon's systems dynamics–based strategy.

With Amazon's retail and marketplace flywheel so core to its business strategy, it's not surprising to learn that it has used a similar flywheel to define its Internet of Things strategy.

The most obvious place to start thinking about your IoT strategy might seem to be with connected devices—the *things* themselves. That would be a mistake. As Bezos told Amazon CTO Werner Vogels at the 2012 AWS conference, his strategy is just the opposite. "We sell our hardware near break-even, so we make money when people USE the device, not when they BUY the device. That is very aligning with customers. It causes us to have the right behaviors." [58] At the time, he was talking about Kindle, but you can see the same strategy play out in IoT, through low-price connected devices like the Echo and Tap.

Much like in retail, it's clear that the big plays in IoT, the ones that could drive billions of dollars of revenue, are not in proprietary connected devices but in providing the infrastructure and tools that will empower other companies and product developers to design, build, and operate their own IoT capabilities. The IoT value chain is defined by devices, connectivity, big data, algorithms, actions, and connection to the rest of the enterprise.

Amazon is creating components that allow customers to create sophisticated, end-to-end data solutions. As a technical developer who uses Amazon Web Services, the more IoT devices you introduce into your IoT system, the more data (both big and small) you will generate. Once you start collecting all that data, you have more and more need for not only Amazon's storage solutions but for its more advanced data toolsets. Amazon's tools and algorithms can help developers both manage and use that data.

Those algorithms give developers useful insights that can help them achieve a business objective. This in turn can help them create more demand for their product and devices. All of these devices and services can be hosted on AWS and use their infrastructure capabilities, leading to greater growth of the infrastructure.

The core Amazon AWS IoT-related services are,

- *AWS S3.* Simple Storage Service is the core cloud-based storage infrastructure, which provides many different tiers of services.
- *Kinesis.* Kinesis facilitates concurrent real-time data-streaming management. In other words, as a business, you can use Kinesis

to process streaming data from thousands of concurrent connected devices and to easily scale up your data management as your business grows.

- *Lambda.* This is service that is ideally suited toward identifying and then running logic (i.e., code) in response to events, at scale and in near real-time basis (millisecond response). Lambda charges customers only when code is executed.
- *Machine Learning.* This is a service with the goal of letting developers without machine-learning backgrounds be able to build machine-learning applications.
- *DynamoDB.* This is Amazon's NoSQL cloud-based database, typically suited for highly scalable, high-performance scenarios.
- *AWS IoT.* This service provides device-to-cloud infrastructure core-management features such as message queuing, authentication, registration, and connection with the above AWS services.
- Amazon also provides other applications to help monitor and manage all of these assets, including CloudWatch and CloudTrail.

All of these AWS services are self-service and on demand, offering "by-the-sip" consumption-based pricing that makes it dramatically easier to build and operate technology at scale. Amazon CTO Verner Vogels has explained that "by leveraging these services, you can build cost-efficient applications that meet the massive scale required for processing the data generated by huge deployments of connected devices."[59]

At this point, the loop looks familiar: more customers lead to lower infrastructure costs, which leads to more customers in the form of services and companies that rely on the infrastructure.

The big bet for Amazon is not creating devices for its retail business but providing cloud infrastructure and software to thousands of companies that need to build IoT devices and capabilities. This is the AWS IoT flywheel and the real business in IoT for Amazon.

Amazon's IoT Flywheel

YOUR IOT-DRIVEN FLYWHEEL BUSINESS MODEL

Connected devices provide the opportunity to extend an enterprise in manners and at a scale that will force a new understanding of the broader industry. As we have outlined through the book, these manners include

- integrating and enabling customer experiences across products and boundaries;
- seeking operational improvements that will reach into the supply chain and vendor base; and
- creating platforms, services, data, and business models much more reliant on partners, vendors, and other actors.

How do you understand all the moving pieces? How do you decide how to prioritize all the potential investments? How do you simply explain to others how all of this fits together and why they should agree?

Taking the time to articulate your flywheel model is one way to tie all of this together and articulate your strategy. There are many books written about systems dynamics, and I encourage you to dive deep. *Thinking in Systems: A Primer* is a good one to start with.

In the meantime, here are the basics I consider when building a systems model.

- *Create a preliminary definition and scope statement of the value chain or scenario.* For example, it could be "Understand the dynamics for my supply chain" or "Achieve greater retention of existing customers." This helps to anchor and put sensible boundaries on the model you're trying to build.
- *Outline the key nouns in the scenario, and put variables to them.* Imagine you're constructing a building ventilation system. You'd need to think through what air-conditioning units, power, thermostats, and insurance companies are involved. You'd also need to consider the variables affected by IoT—increased revenue from air-conditioning units, improved power efficiency, decreased insurance costs or risks, and so forth. Those are the actors with relationships between them; they'll either feed into each other or work against each other. A full understanding of all of the actors or variables will help you think through the dynamics and interplay among all of the actors in the system.
- *Rationalize and group the nouns and variables.* Simplify the nouns into groups that seem to all be the same thing or variables of the same thing. In building the Amazon IoT flywheel model, I grouped all the AWS solutions into the "big-data solutions" variable. It's essential to organize the variables in a system at the right level so that you understand which work together and which function more separately. This will also keep you from dealing with too many variables at any one time—you want to generally be dealing with at most ten to twenty variables at any one time. You're creating the level of abstraction.
- *Build the causal-relationship diagram.* These identify the cause-and-effect relationships between variables, giving insights to the feedback loops, unintended consequences, timing between effects, and relationships. Does increasing or decreasing this

variable increase or decrease another variable? If the answer is no, they're not really connected. If the answer is yes, you'll need to determine whether it's a positive or negative, decreasing relationship. Does it apply positive pressure from one variable to the other or negative pressure? For example, the more sellers you have selling the same or similar products, that applies a negative pressure to, or decreases, prices.

- *Keep working at it, and simplify.* You will likely need several sessions and a couple of versions. Going through this multiple times will help a leadership team build a common understanding of the business and the levers of the business. Once you have a basic model, you may also need to include different variations of your model (a higher level, or "zoom in"). You might also build both a current version and a yet-to-be version of your flywheel.

- *Identify the implications of the model.* Once you understand the relationships between variables, then you need to take a step back and think about the unique role your company might play in this model. How do we get the flywheel spinning? What are the investments? What are the risks? What are the opportunities? How do we create leverage and energy? What are the synergies, and what's the best way for us to create these synergies? How are competitor actions mapping against this flywheel? A flywheel tends to keep itself spinning once you get it spinning. If you put energy into certain aspects of the model, it will create a virtuous cycle.

The value of creating your own flywheel is threefold: Gain a deeper and broader understanding of your industry that includes opportunities, risks, and dead zones. Define your strategy, and prioritize specific actions. Create a model that will help you communicate this strategy to others.

How long will building out your flywheel take? Longer than you might think. If you haven't had a few aha moments, then you're likely not digging deep enough.

Six Steps to Designing Your Own Flywheel

1 Create a preliminary definition and scope statement

2 Outline the key nouns and variables

3 Rationalize and group the nouns and variables

4 Build a causal relationship diagram

5 Keep working the model and simplify overtime

6 Identify the implications of the model

■ ■ ■

You've now learned all ten principles of using IoT to impact your business—from how IoT is being used to build the next generation of Amazon's customer obsession to creating new business models using IoT.

In the final section of this book, I'll walk you through how to use the ten Internet of Things principles we've learned already to build a better set of plans for your IoT strategy. Feel free to look back and reference specific principles throughout the rest of the book as you go.

Conclusion: Developing Your IoT Strategy and Plan

Beware of the man who knows the answer
before he understands the question.

—ANONYMOUS

It was a dreary February early morning in 1999 in Portland, Oregon, and my good friend and longtime mentor, Steve Maupin, and I had just delivered an inspiring, value-building, and compelling integrated-supply-chain and manufacturing strategy to the senior leadership team of a forest-products company.

The CEO, at the surface a crusty forest-products operator but at his heart a sophisticated sales and operating executive, sat back after the presentation. Steve and I, standing up front, waited with the rest of his leadership team in silence. We had been retained to do an enterprise planning resource (ERP) software selection for his company and, as part of this, had built this integrated-supply-chain strategy.

The CEO looked up and, slowly, without emotion, started. "I drove in this morning in a good mood. I went and saw a baseball game with my son last night. Business is good. So I'm trying to understand why I'm so mad right now." He turned to Steve and me.

"Have you ever heard the term RTFP?" he inquired.

Steve and I shook our heads no.

"RTFP stands for 'read the f—— problem.' If I had wanted an integrated-supply-chain strategy, I would have asked for one." What he was really looking for, or so he thought, was a software strategy, and so we quickly went on to the software-selection part of the agenda.

Steve and I laugh about this term, RTFP, and story. In the case of the forest-products CEO, we hadn't worked hard enough to help him see the opportunity and the connection between the software he wanted and the integrated-supply-chain strategy we presented. These days we often refer to RTFP when collaborating on a client situation—usually in terms of how to help our clients start a project off with better questions. This notion of how to ask better questions has become foundational in how I attack problems.

In the course of my career, I've estimated and planned hundreds of projects. I've learned that, even before you start seeking answers, it's imperative to understand the questions. Guiding a team to a successful outcome on a complex project requires understanding of the steps and deliverables, necessary resources, and roles and every inherent risk and dependency.

Before starting the hardware and software design, before figuring out how to engage developers, before planning the launch party, you should start with a better set of questions.

In this section of the book, I'll outline the set of tools that have helped Amazon and I ask the right questions to think through and plan IoT businesses. We'll talk about how to apply these tools and strategies to your business and how to use them to build your own understanding, communicate your vision to your team, and identify the requirements and next steps for your IoT business.

A note on sequencing: Though I've outlined all of the following steps as sequential, they're often actually done concurrently, and there are many ways to approach them. I've outlined them here in the most likely progression, which I feel helps lead to a top-down development of insights, but don't feel trapped by the order.

I recommend using the checklist located at the end of this book to help you guide and keep track of your IoT planning. I've included an example for some of the tools, but it is easy to find examples and tutorials on all of these tools in books and online.

As you build your plans, remember that though IoT can provide key pieces to the puzzle, it's no golden ticket. Simply creating an IoT solution will not bring you success. However, if you focus on providing strong value to your customers through new or updated products and services, improving company operations, or creating new or more-efficient business models, you'll be much more likely to find success.

It might be obvious to you where the IoT opportunities lie in your business. You may see clearly how to proceed; that the organizational implications are minimal; that the work to be done is mostly technology oriented. If that's the situation you are in, there's a chance you should proceed directly to *go*, collect your funding, and enable a smart device.

But in most circumstances, to lay the right foundation, understand the breadth of the opportunity, and develop understanding and support in the organization, there is work to be done before proceeding to construction.

PART 1. DEVELOP AND ARTICULATE YOUR STRATEGY

Michael Porter, professor of strategy at Harvard, has said that "the essence of strategy is choosing what not to do."[60] In the wide array of opportunities you likely have with IoT, narrowing and prioritizing is the first step. The point of this first set of exercises is to allow you to narrow smartly by developing an understanding of the market and deliberate evaluation of your opportunities. Doing this work up front will allow for more scale and sophistication.

1. *Landscape Analysis.* Drawing up a thorough analysis of your industry, competitors, strengths, weaknesses, opportunities, and threats (SWOT) will help you understand the backdrop, the megatrends, and the forces at play in your market. Understanding these factors will set the stage for a successful IoT play through heightened awareness of threats and weaknesses. But the landscape analysis also feeds into a deeper understanding—dare I say obsession—with your customers and their environment.

2. *Value-Chain Analysis and Profit-Pool Analysis.* Next up is creating your value-chain analysis and profit-pool analysis for your industry. Make this a broad view of the industry, not just a narrow view of your current business. You'll remember Amazon's deliberate "launch and learn" strategy from principle 9: Launch a business in one part of the value chain, and then use that opportunity to

learn about the rest of the value chain and identify other possible business opportunities. Although we didn't produce an explicit value-chain analysis, working this way taught us all the lessons we might have learned if we had.

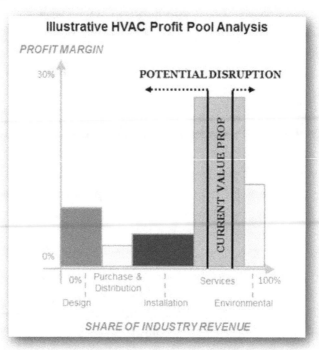

3. *Partner, Competitor, and Vendor Analysis.* It's amazing what you can learn about what's going on in your industry on a topic like IoT by creating a map of other solutions providers in the space. You should use this exercise to develop a clear understanding of what exactly each does, who their key clients are, and what their use cases are in the IoT landscape. You should also pick a few to interview. This is helpful preliminary work in developing a plan for partners and vendor selection. It's also a less direct route to Amazon's first leadership principle, which you'll remember is customer obsession. Understanding partners, competitors, and vendors will help you begin to see the needs of your customers,

the smart way those needs are already being met, and the gaps in the way those needs are currently being met. As we'd say at Amazon, "It's OK to use other people's good ideas that weren't invented here."

4. *Customer Needs.* Developing customer personas and mapping those customers' current journeys is a great way to document specific unmet needs and identify key friction points your future customers are experiencing right now. Following the path from start to your desired outcome can help you identify details and priorities that might otherwise be dealt with at too high a level or skipped over entirely.

    Crafting strong customer personas and journeys is hard work. It's likely you'll need to iterate a few times before you really nail them. (I oftentimes need to start over more than once before I gain any real insights.) The biggest mistake you can make on these is to build them for show rather than for work. Don't worry about the beauty of these deliverables until things are getting baked (if at all). Do worry about getting at insights, talking to customers, and validating your findings with others who can bring insights and challenges to your work.

5. *Evaluation Framework and Scoring.* The next step in the process is to design the ways in which you will assess the success of your work. This includes understanding a project's feasibility and transition points and how it will tie into other corporate strategies at your company. Sometimes, especially if your organization is new to the field of connected devices, the success of your project should be measured in terms of what you can learn from the project rather than whether or not it can be classically considered a success. In this case, evaluate for situations that can present lower risk of impact if "failure" occurs. Remember, failure is great, as long as the impact can contained and minimized. Some of your early initiatives may be purely to gain experience with no expected ROI.

6. *Strategy Articulation.* Once you've done all of these analyses, it's time to articulate your learning to the rest of your team. Like the rest of these steps, there are many possible ways to articulate your proposed strategy, but there are two in particular that I have found to be most effective in clarifying and communicating strategy—building a flywheel model of your business systems and articulating a business model.

CONSTRUCTING YOUR FLYWHEEL MODEL
A flywheel, or systems-dynamic model, helps identify, validate, and communicate the ways that the different forces and dynamics in your business are connected. It helps you understand whether those forces reinforce or work against each other.

One of the benefits of working hard on a flywheel model is that it will help you either see opportunities or identify competitive risks in the industry or scenario you're considering. It will help you understand how to overcome inertia and create momentum, establishing reinforcing feedback loops along the way.

"Companies that pursue a flywheel-business model focus on building the kind of long-term capabilities that allow them to prevail against rivals and capture new opportunities for growth."[61] Before you get started, I recommend rereading principle 10 for a full description of how to go about creating your own flywheel model.

ARTICULATING YOUR BUSINESS MODEL
In my experience, the most logical next step after creating a flywheel model is to dive into the development of your business model. I like to use a business-model canvas or template to articulate and explain the many facets of a business model. These template-driven approaches help a small team quickly think through broad issues. They are fun and easy to facilitate and help keep energy high as you build an iterative and appropriate level of documentation.

To help clarify and explain important differences between options that I'm thinking about, I typically develop multiple business-model canvases. They're a great way to outline and clarify minor differences between partnering models and revenue models and identify key choices around building or partnering on platform components that you're considering.

Business Model Generation, by Alexander Osterwalder and Yves Pigneur, is a great source for both standard and in-depth business-model templates. For IoT-focused business models, you'll need to adapt these models. I recommend using the following questions to adapt Osterwalder and Pigneur's models for IoT-centric opportunities:

- What data would be valuable if a sensor could collect it?
- What efficiency or valuable insight could be developed by an algorithm (don't focus too much on the feasibility yet)?
- What add-on or new services or insights could be developed? Are there new customer opportunities?
- How could ecosystem partners (oftentimes software and solution developers) help in both distribution and capabilities development and differentiation?
- What are the potential revenue models for a given business model?

Once you've designed your flywheel and business model, it's time to get company leadership on board with your plan. It's important that they be both well informed and supportive of your plan if you want it to succeed.

From there, it's time to build your IoT Roadmap.

PART 2: BUILD YOUR IOT ROADMAP

Where strategy articulation helps you explain what the big idea is and why you should do it, the IoT roadmap helps you plan and communicate to others what the journey will be like to get there and add clarity to exactly what is being built and how it will work.

In creating your roadmap, embrace one of Amazon's favorite strategies—think big, but bet small. Here's a reminder of the leadership principle explored in my first book: "Thinking small is a self-fulfilling prophecy. Leaders create and communicate a bold vision that inspires results. They think differently and look around corners for ways to serve customers."[62]

But don't confuse "thinking big" with "betting big." Once you have a big vision, you'll need to make a small bet to test your thinking. This is particularly true if your fully implemented ideas would have a big impact on existing customer experience or products or if they would shift your business model. A prototype that's lower risk in terms of financial or operational risk can allow you test a big opportunity, theory, or idea. Be iterative, build prototypes, and fail fast.

Companies that do this well will out-innovate those that don't. A prototype isn't the only way to test this—creating minimally viable products or jointly developing a project with your existing customers and partners are also good options for minimizing the size of your bet and making experimentation more feasible.

Here are a four specific ways that teams at Amazon might think differently about kick-starting their IoT programs. Each step will clarify your strategy and build toward a greater understanding of what success might look like. By articulating the specifics of your future success clearly, you will also help your team understand the specifics of what it would to get there.

THE FUTURE PRESS RELEASE: DEVELOPING AN ORGANIZED VISION

Bezos is famous for requiring teams to create a "future press release" before launching into a new product, undergoing any kind of transformation, or entering a new market. Going through the process of creating a simple but specific product announcement forces you to find clarity around your vision. You have to think through key features and adoption and weigh your project's likely path to success. Putting all of this down in a press release, speculative though it may be, also helps you express these things more clearly to important stakeholders. We used this future-press-release approach at Amazon, and it has been a consistent tool I use with clients. They really love it.

The future press release is a great approach to define clear and lofty goals, requirements, and objectives and build broad understanding from the start of a program or enterprise change. There are, however, rules to make this approach effective:

Rule 1. The goal must be stated at a future point in time where success has been achieved and realized. Press releases at launch are good, but a better one is sometime after launch, where true success can be discussed.

Rule 2. Use the release to explain why the product is important, oftentimes to customers (or other key stakeholders). Discuss the accomplishments in terms of why it is important to customers. How did the customer experience improve? Why does the customer care? Then discuss other reasons it was important and key goals.

Rule 3. Set an audacious and clear goal. Articulate clear measurable results you've achieved, including financial, operating, and market share results.

Rule 4. Outline the principles used that led to success. This is the trickiest and most important aspect of the future press release. Outline the hard things accomplished, the important decisions, and the design principles that led to success. Discuss the issues that needed to be addressed to achieve success. Getting the "tricky" issues on the table early on helps everyone understand the real nature of change needed. Don't worry about discussing how to solve these issues yet. You've still got time to figure that out.

Once you've created a future press release, the project leader needs to be empowered to make these changes happen. Focus on creating a future press release oriented communication plan that helps that project leader find success across the organization.

The future press release is a type of forcing function. Once the press release is reviewed and approved, teams have a difficult time backing out of the commitments made. A leader can refer to many parts of the press release and use it to remind and hold teams accountable. It paints a clear vision to galvanize understanding and commitment.

AN FAQ FOR YOUR IOT PLAN

Once you've written a press release, you can forecast some of the questions you're likely to get about your product in a frequently asked questions, or FAQ, document. The purpose of the FAQ is to add more details to the press release and answer other business and execution questions necessary to launch. This can be either a separate document or appended to the end of your future press release.

By proactively writing an FAQ, you're forcing yourself to think through what the key questions about your product will be and helping to answer the big questions your stakeholders are likely to have.

A good FAQ allows the press release document to stay short and focused on what the customer gets. The FAQ should include resolution and answers to issues and questions that come up when you are writing the press release. It should also respond to questions that arise through the process of socializing the press release. A good FAQ includes questions that define what the product is good for, how it will be leveraged by the customer, and why it will delight the customer.

The FAQ forces you to put yourself in the role of the customer using the product and consider all the challenges or confusions you might have. It also provides inspiration for designing a fully self-service, confusion-free product.

USER MANUAL—START WITH THE END IN MIND

Developing a preliminary user manual for your IoT device can be a powerful tool early on in a project. We used this at Amazon when developing products or APIs. Your IoT user manual should address at least two key customer segments.

1. *The End User of the IoT Device.* Who is the customer that will be installing, using, adjusting, and getting feedback from your IoT

product? Outline what the unpacking directions will be, what the installation process will be, how updates will happen, what the data privacy terms will be, how to use and read the device, and how to connect it. Think through all the major steps the users of the product will need to take, and include them in a close-to-real-life user manual. Forcing to keep these steps simple will lead to great product ideas, user experience, and technology design.

2. *The Programmer Developing to Your IoT Device and API.* If your IoT product will include an API allowing developers to access, deploy, integrate, and extend your product, then you'll also want to build a user manual for the developer. Write out the interface for the API, what events will be supported, and the data to be sent and received. Give example code snippets and outline key operational topics such as how testing occurs and how operational status and updates are facilitated. You'll also want to use this exercise to outline key business and use terms. Are there charges involved?

As you can see, all of these techniques strive for three things:

1. Breadth of thinking through use cases and requirements
2. Clarity around the experience—what it will be, how it will work, and what it will provide
3. Simplicity to drive easy-to-use products

PROJECT CHARTER

A project charter is a written project overview outlining the key facets of a project. The project charter is the part of the IoT roadmap that helps you take what you've decided to do and put it into action: What resources will you need to make this happen? What are the key milestones? What's the schedule for accomplishing these things? Often, project managers rely solely on GANTT charts to plan a project. The project charter adds other topics and nuance to the planning process.

Planning starts with the process of taking ideas and strategies and articulating how you will go about the objectives of the project. Deeper project plans will oftentimes be appropriate, but the project charter is a lean approach to project planning and estimating. It's essentially the ninety-day plan for what you'll do to get your project going. I developed this template over many years of scoping and communicating projects to a diverse set of stakeholders. The key elements of the project charter are as follows:

- *Project Objective.* The simple and minimal description of the initiative and why it matters. This can be the "elevator" speech for describing a project and why it is valuable.
- *Initiative Description and Deliverables.* A deeper breakdown of the objective and discussion of the high-level deliverables to be created through the life of the project.
- *Major Milestone.* Using the description and deliverables, outline key milestones for the initiative.
- *Team.* Who are the people, and what are roles needed for the initiative? Place focus first on the full-time resources needed and then on other contributors. Focus on the roles needed to actually do the work versus roles to review the work.
- *Metrics/Measures/Goals.* Articulate the quantifiable goals for the initiative. Focus on customer-oriented measures wherever possible and then business-impact measures. These are not metrics for the project itself but instead tied to the impact this capability will have.
- *Assumptions and Dependencies.* What are the critical capabilities, organizations, projects, and so forth that are critical to the success of this initiative? These are often "unproven" or still in delivery, but identifying them outright will help to flag places you may want to be thoughtful in facilitating collaboration throughout the initiative.

Many issues in a project emerge due to a lack of clarity—"I thought you meant this" is a refrain you don't want to hear during a project. By diving deep into dependencies early in the project planning phase, you can hopefully avoid these kinds of issues coming up later on in the project.

As leaders at Amazon, we were carefully coached to avoid these kinds of surprises. The fourteenth leadership principle, deliver results, instructs company leadership to "focus on the key inputs for their business and deliver them with the right quality and in a timely fashion. Despite setbacks, they rise to the occasion and never settle."

While planning key initiatives, we were focused on our dependencies. In most cases, those dependencies were teams and capabilities we were not in direct control of but that were critical to our results. We often received lectures about "managing our dependencies" as a way to remind us of the risks in our delivery plans. Dive deep into your dependencies, and outline the schedules, risks, metrics, and critical aspects.

- *Risks.* Articulate the most critical risks to delivering this vision. I recommend not repeating items already listed as "assumptions and dependencies" section. This is not a "cover your ass" (CYA) exercise but a value-oriented process to help identify and communicate risks and what might be done to either avoid, mitigate, or accept.
- *Duration.* For this first leg of the journey, start estimating and setting expectations for the duration and potential range.
- *Budget.* Identify the typical spend and real budget needed for this project: tools, facilities, expenses, contractor, and consultant spend and perhaps initial marketing or communications are key categories.

The beauty of this "project-on-a-page" template is that it gives a well-balanced view of what the project is. It's a useful tool not only for developing your own understanding of the project but to use as a consistent reminder of the project's principles to everyone involved.

PART 3. IDENTIFY AND MAP YOUR IOT REQUIREMENTS

The last step in creating your IoT roadmap is to create a set of IoT requirements—the technical capabilities you'll need to put in place to make your solution a success. Using and referencing your charter, the creation of which we outlined above in part 2, will help you develop the requirements of what you're going to build.

Companies use many different types of approaches, such as use cases, user stories, process flows, personas, architecture specifications, and so on to document their requirements. Regardless of the requirements methodology you use, I have found that considering and answering the following set of questions is an important part of building IoT capabilities or solutions. You might be able to specify requirements just by answering these questions.

Insights (Data and Events)

- What problem, event, or insight is the end user solving for?
- What insights would be valuable to the customer?
- What recommendation or optimization using the data would be valuable to a customer?
- What risks or nonconforming situations might impact the customer? How could your product, perhaps partnering with other devices, identify these risks?
- What data needs to be collected?
- How often does it need to be collected?
- What types of events, forecasts, or "optimizations" could be identified or derived from sensors and data?
- Does the data need to be combined with any data or events not resident at the device?
- Will data and events be combined across devices?
- Who else (users, devices) will subscribe to the data?

Analytics and Recommendations

- How responsive will "adjustments" or optimizations need to be (specify in time range)?
- How complex will the "math" be? Write the math equation or pseudologic code if you can.

- Will notifications, logic, "math," or algorithms be consistent and fixed, or will they need to be configurable, updated, and managed?
- Who else (users, devices) will subscribe to the analytics? Who needs to be notified of events, data, or analysis of data from the device (or devices)?
- How will they be notified?

Performance

- Estimate the amount of data transmitted over a period of time (hour, day).
- What are the consequences of data not be collected?
- What are the consequences of data being collected but not transmitted?
- What are the consequences of the device not being connected?
- How quick (in seconds) do alerts or adjustments need to be received by the device?
- How quick (in seconds) do alerts or adjustments need to be received by other subscribers?
- How close will the devices collecting data or subscribing to analytics be to each other?

Environment and Operating Requirements

- What operating conditions will the device and sensor be in? Temperature, moisture, pressure, access, and vibration are example conditions.
- What device physical-security needs or risks are there?
- Will the IoT device or sensors be embedded within another device, or will they be independent and a primary physical device themselves?
- How will the IoT device connect?
- How constant does the connection need to be?
- How reliable does the connection need to be?

Costs

- What is the cost per device target range?
- What is the cost per device for connectivity target range?
- What is the additional operating cost range the business can support for ongoing operating infrastructure?

Once you've completed all of your IoT roadmap deliverables—including developing and articulating each component of your IoT strategy and then creating your IoT roadmap—you will have all the essential elements you need to get to work building your IoT capability.

At this point, you know what you want to accomplish, you know why you want to accomplish it, and you even have an idea of how you want to accomplish it. Now, go accomplish it. Or as Yoda said, "There is only do or do not. There is no try."

ALWAYS BE STRIVING

The death knell for any enterprise is to glorify the past—
no matter how good it was.

—Jeff Bezos

If you're fortunate, the innovative IoT-enabled operational improvement or business strategy is obvious and well accepted across the organization, and you have the leadership support to drive all aspects of change necessary for success. For the other 99.9 percent of us, there's hard work to do to develop the idea, build understanding, create the right environment for change, and get all the leadership alignment needed.

This chapter and the entire book have outlined some of the techniques that can be used to do this in a nimble, iterative manner. It's OK if you've started with the technology and now are coming around to the business and change strategy—change is messy and doesn't usually progress in a logical or ideal manner.

But why is innovation so hard? Why is a company like Amazon rated as a singular standout by analysts and peers as the number-one supply-chain company for being both operationally excellent and innovative?[63] Why is challenging the status quo so difficult? I believe the answer lies deep within our fears. I'm talking in particular about the fear of failure, especially once you are successful. The fear of breaking traditions.

In 2013, the TV commentator Charlie Rose did an interview with Jeff Bezos.[64] In discussing why Amazon is constantly pushing to invent new businesses, Bezos said the following: "Companies have short life spans and Amazon will be disrupted one day. I don't worry about it because I know it is inevitable. Companies come and go. Companies that are the shiniest and most important of any era and you just wait a couple of decades and they are gone. I would love for it [Amazon's disruption] to be after I'm dead."

Companies that don't let their past models and success define who they are will be those that span eras and define what comes next. A new era is upon us—the era of connected devices, driven by sensors, abundant connectivity, cloud computing, and machine learning.

Will you challenge your status quo and traditions to seize the opportunity of the IoT era?

A Checklist for Developing Your Internet of Things Strategy

The list below is outlined to help you keep track of the many components of a successful Internet of Things plan. I hope you'll use this to track your progress as you develop your own strategy. I also invite you to share your questions, your progress, and your own learnings on my blog at www. on-amzn.com.

Part 1. Develop and Articulate Your Strategy

1. Create a landscape analysis
2. Create value-chain and profit-pool analyses
3. Create partner, competitor and vendor analyses
4. Identify customer needs
5. Create evaluation framework
6. Articulate your strategy
   a. Build your flywheel model
   b. Create your business model

Part 2. Build Your IoT Roadmap

1. Small but informative starts
   a. Write a future press release
   b. Create an FAQ
   c. Create a user manual
2. Build a project charter
   a. Project objective
   b. Initiative description and deliverables
   c. Major milestone
   d. Team
   e. Metrics, measures, and goals
   f. Assumptions and dependencies

g. Risks
h. Duration
i. Budget

Part 3. Identify and Map Your IoT Requirements

1. Insights (data and events)
2. Analytics and recommendations
3. Performance
4. Environment and operating requirements
5. Costs

Endnotes

1. Gartner, "Gartner Says 6.4 Billlion Connected 'Things' Will Be in Use in 2016, Up 30 Percent From 2015," News release, November 10, 2015, http://www.gartner.com/newsroom/id/3165317.

2. Manyika, James, Michael Chui, Peter Bisson, Jonathan Woetzel, Richard Dobbs, Jacques Bughin, and Dan Aharon, "The Internet of Things: Mapping the Value Beyond the Hype," *Mickinsey&Company*, June 2015.

3. Michael Porter and James Helppelmann, "How Smart, Connected Products are Transforming Competition," *Harvard Business Review*, November, 2014, https://hbr.org/2014/11/how-smart-connected-products-are-transforming-competition.

4. "Steve Jobs' 2005 Stanford Commencement Address." Youtube viedo, 15:04. From Stanford. Posted by Stanford March 7, 2008. https://www.youtube.com/watch?v=UF8uR6Z6KLc.

5. Daniel B. Kline, "How Many Prime Members Does Amazon Have (And Why It Matters)," *The Motley Fool*, January 26, 2016, http://www.fool.com/investing/general/2016/01/26/how-many-prime-members-does-amazon-have-and-why-it.aspx.

6. Zoe Chace, "Why Amazon Loses Money on Every Kindle Fire," *NPR*, November 15, 2011, http://www.npr.org/sections/money/2011/11/16/142310104/why-amazon-loses-money-on-every-kindle-fire.

7. Sabrina Korber, "Retail's 'Beacon of Hope: Shopping That's Personal," *CNBC*, May 26, 2015, http://www.cnbc.com/2015/05/26/retails-newest-brick-and-mortar-bet.html.

8. "What's driving the connected car," *McKinsey&Company*, September 2014, http://www.mckinsey.com/industries/automotive-and-assembly/our-insights/whats-driving-the-connected-car..

9. Marc Wulfraat, "Amazon Global Fulfillment Center Network," *MWPVL International*, August 2016, http://www.mwpvl.com/html/amazon_com.html.

10. Alex Jablokow, "How the IoT Keeps Oil and Gas Pipelines Safe," *PTC*, November 3, 2015, http://blogs.ptc.com/2015/11/03/how-the-iot-helps-keep-oil-and-gas-pipelines-safe/.

11. Jeffrey R Immelt, "GE 2015 Annual Report," *GE*, February 26, 2016, http://www.ge.com/ar2015/letter/.

12. Pedro Domingo, *The Master Algorithm*, (New York: Basic Books, 2015).

13. Daniel Price, "Facts and Stats About the Big Data Industry," *Cloud Tweaks*, March 17, 2015, http://cloudtweaks.com/2015/03/surprising-facts-and-stats-about-the-big-data-industry/.

14. From multiple Amazon job listings.

15. "Amazon Mechanical Turk FAQ," last modified 2016, https://www.mturk.com/mturk/help?helpPage=overview.

16. Werner Vogel, April 27, 2011 (12:51 a.m.), Jeff Bezos Letter, "The Amazon.com 2010 Shareholder Letter Focusses on Technology," http://www.allthingsdistributed.com/2011/04/the_amazon-com_2010_shareholder.html.

17. Steve Rosenbush, "The Morning Dowload: Amazon CFO Says Algoithm-Based Decision Making Helped Company Achieve

Profit," *The Wall Street Journal*, July 24, 2015, http://blogs.wsj.com/ cio/2015/07/24/the-morning-download-amazon-cfo-says-algorithm-based-decision-making-helped-company-achieve-profit/.

18. Peggy Hollinger, "Meet the Cobots: Humans and Robots Together on the Factory Floor," *Financial Times*, May 5, 2016, https://next.ft.com/ content/6d5d609e-02e2-11e6-af1d-c47326021344.

19. Kevin Kruse, "How to be innovative: 6 secrets from Jeff Bezos," *CEO. com*, July 23, 2013, http://www.ceo.com/technology_and_innovation/ how-to-be-innovative-6-secrets-from-jeff-bezos/.

20. Jeff Bezos, "2015 Letter to Shareholders," Amazon.com, 2015, http:// phx.corporate-ir.net/phoenix.zhtml?c=97664&p=irol-SECText&TEX T=aHR0cDovL2FwaS50ZW5rd2l6YXJkLmNvbS9maWxpbmcueG1sP 2lwYWdlPTEwODYwMjA1JkRTRVE9MCZTRVE9MCZTUURFU0M9U-0VDVElPTI9FTlRJUkUkmc3Vic2lkPTU3.

21. "Interview: Amazon CEO Jeff Bezos." Youtube video, 52:53. From Business Insider's Ignition 2014. Posted by Business Insider, December 15, 2014. https://www.youtube.com/watch?v=Xx92bUw7WX8.

22. Gartner, "The Gartner Supply Chain Top 25 for 2015," News release, May 14, 2015, http://www.gartner.com/newsroom/id/3053118.

23. Maxwell Wessel, "Why Big Companies Can't Innovate," *Harvard Business Review*, September 27, 2012, https://hbr.org/2012/09/ why-big-companies-cant-innovate.

24. Taylor Soper, " Amazon's Secrets of Invention: Jeff Bezos Explains How to Build an Innovative Team," *Geekwire*, May 27, 2016, http:// www.geekwire.com/2016/amazons-secrets-invention-jeff-bezos-explains-build-innovative-team/.

25. Jason Del Rey, "Meet the Guy Behind Amazon's Secret Retail Store Plans," *Recode*, February 3, 2016, http://recode.net/2016/02/03/ meet-the-guy-behind-amazons-secret-retail-store-plans/.

26. Phil Wahba, "This Chart Shows Just How Dominant Amazon Is," *Fortune*, November 6, 2015, http://fortune.com/2015/11/06/amazon-retailers-ecommerce/.

27. Marc Andresssen, "The Three Kinds of Platforms You Meet on the Internet," *blog.pmarca.com*, http://pmarchive.com/three_kinds_of_ platforms_you_meet_on_the_internet.html.

28. "This Lesser-Known Amazon Business Is Growing Fast," *Fortune*, January 5, 2016, http://fortune.com/2016/01/05/amazon-sellers-holidays/.

29. Napier Lopez, "Amazon's Alexa Voice Service Is Now Open for Third-Parties to Use in Their Products," *TNW*, September 12, 2015, http:// thenextweb.com/gadgets/2015/06/25/amazons-alexa-voice-service-is-now-open-for-third-parties-to-use-in-their-products/ #gref.

30. "Amazon Opens Alexa Voice Serice to Third Party Hardward Makers," News release, June 25, 2015, http://phx.corporate-ir.net/phoenix. zhtml?c=176060&p=irol-newsArticle&ID=2062557..

31. Peter Kafka, "Eric Schmidt's 'Gang of Four' Doesn't Have Room for Microsoft," *All Things D*, May 31, 2011, http://allthingsd.com/20110531/ eric-schmidts-gang-of-four-doesnt-have-room-for-microsoft/.

32. Phil Simon, *The Age of the Platform: How Amazon, Apple, Facebook and Google Have Redefined Business* (Motion Publishing, 2011).

33. "Amazon Dash Replenishment." Youtube video, 1:35. From Amazon Dash Replenishment Service. Posted by Amazon Dash

Replenishment Service January 19, 2016, https://www.youtube.com/watch?v=vTYcWG6BIDY.

34. John Greenough, "From Fitness Trackers to Drones, How the Internet of Things is Transforming the Insurance Industry," *Business Insider India*, July 6, 2015, http://www.businessinsider.in/From-fitness-trackers-to-drones-how-the-Internet-of-Things-is-transforming-the-insurance-industry/articleshow/47964479.cms.

35. "Zipcar," last modified September 10, 2016, https://en.wikipedia.org/wiki/Zipcar.

36. Craig Powers, "Using the Internet of Things to Provide 'Air-as-a-Service,'"*ASUGNews*, June 25th, 2015, http://www.asugnews.com/article/internet-of-things-kaeser-example.

37. Beth Stackpole, "IoT-Enabled Product as a Service Could Transform Manufacturing," TechTarget, April, 2015, http://internetofthingsagenda.techtarget.com/feature/IoT-enabled-product-as-a-service-could-transform-manufacturing.

38. Christopher Mines, Michele Pelino, Charles S Golvin, Holger Kisker, Sharyn Leaver, Joanna Clark, "Mapping the Connected World," *Forrester* (2013): 12.

39. Oliver Staley, "Amazon is Hiring the Most MBAs in Tech and It's Not Really Close," *Quartz*, March 14, 2016, http://qz.com/636539/amazon-is-hiring-the-most-mbas-in-tech-and-its-not-really-close/.

40. Douglas Laney, Alan D. Duncan, Mario Faria, Debra Logan, Alan Dayley, Guido De Simoni, Michael Patrick Moran, Andrew White, and Saul Judah, "Predicts 2016: Information Strategy," *Gartner* (2015). ID: G00293176.

41. Kevin Werbach, "Syndication: The Emerging Model for Business in the Internet Era," *Harvard Business Review*, May-June 2000 Issue, https://hbr.org/2000/05/syndication-the-emerging-model-for-business-in-the-internet-era.

42. Romain Dillet, "Nest Uses Its Data to Turn Electric Utilities into Cash Cows," *TechCrunch*, April 18, 2014, http://techcrunch.com/2014/04/18/nest-uses-its-data-to-turn-electric-utilities-into-cash-cows/.

43. Larry Zhou, "How Zappos Uses Third-Party Info like Weather Data to Better Personalize Ads," *Venture Beat*, August 5, 2014, http://venturebeat.com/2014/08/05/how-zappos-uses-third-party-info-like-weather-data-better-personalize-ads/.

44. "Farm Bureau Survey: Farmers Want to Control Their Own Data," *The Voice of Agriculture*, May 11, 2016, http://www.fb.org/newsroom/news_article/429/.

45. Willie Vogt, "Data Concerns Remain Top of Mind for Farmers," *Farm Industry News*, May 12, 2016, http://farmindustrynews.com/farm-equipment/data-concerns-remain-top-mind-farmers.

46. "International Safe Harbor Privacy Principles," last modified September 7, 2016, https://en.wikipedia.org/wiki/International_Safe_Harbor_Privacy_Principles.

47. "Facebook Hit with Fresh Challenve to Its European Operations," *Fortune*, May 25, 2016, http://fortune.com/2016/05/25/facebook-data-transfers/

48. Kim S. Nash "CIOs Consider Putting a Price Tag on Data," *CIO.com*, June 23, 2014, http://www.cio.com/article/2375573/leadership-management/cios-consider-putting-a-price-tag-on-data.html.

49. "Nasdaq: Amazon.com," 2016, http://www.4-traders.com/AMAZON-COM-4846/financials/.

50. Brian Deagon, " Amazon Price Target Hiked Based on Savings From New Airline Fleet," *Investor's Business Daily*, June 16, 2016, http://www.investors.com/news/technology/amazon-price-target-hiked-based-on-savings-from-new-airline-fleet/.

51. Jeff Bezos, "2016 Letter to Shareholders," *Amazon.com*, 2016, https://www.sec.gov/Archives/edgar/data/1018724/000119312515144741/d895323dex991.htm.

52. "Amazon's Jeff Bezos: The Ultimate Disrupter," *Fortune*, December 3, 2012, http://fortune.com/2012/11/16/amazons-jeff-bezos-the-ultimate-disrupter/.

53. Orit Gadiesh and James L. Gilbert, "How to Map Your Industry's Profit Pool," *Harvard Business Review*, May-June 1998 Issue, https://hbr.org/1998/05/how-to-map-your-industrys-profit-pool.

54. Jeff Bezos, "2014 Letter to Shareholders," Amazon.com, 2014, https://www.sec.gov/Archives/edgar/data/1018724/000119312515144741/d895323dex991.htm

55. Bezos, "2016 Letter to Shareholder."

56. FIND EVERTHING STORE PAGE NUMBER

57. John Cook, "Jeff Bezos on Innovation" Amazon 'Willing to Be Misunderstood for Long Periods of Time,'" *GeekWire*, June7, 2011, http://www.geekwire.com/2011/amazons-bezos-innovation/.

58. Robert Hof, "Jeff Bezos: How Amazon Web Services Is Just like the Kindle Business," *Forbes*, November 29, 2012, http://www.forbes.

com/sites/roberthof/2012/11/29/jeff-bezos-how-amazon-web-services-is-just-like-the-kindle-business/#293835b051b3.

59. Daniel Robinson, "Amazon Pushes 'Serverless' Cloud Services Using AWS Lambda," *V3*, June 14, 2016, http://www.v3.co.uk/v3-uk/news/2461473/amazon-pushes-serverless-cloud-services-using-aws-lambda.

60. Joan Magretta, "Jim Collins, Meet Michael Porter," *Harvard Business Review*, December 15, 2011, https://hbr.org/2011/12/jim-collins-meet-michael-porte.

61. Peter, August 6, 2013, shared article by Tim Laseter and Jeff Bennett "Building a Flywheel Business," *Blog Spot*, May 28, 2013, http://petersposting.blogspot.com/2013/08/building-flywheel-business.html.

62. "Leadership Principles," https://www.amazon.jobs/principles.

63. Stan Aronow, Michael Burkett, Kimberly Niles, and Jim Romano, The Gartner Supply Chain Top 25 for 2015," *Gartner* (2015). ID: G00276456.

64. Charlie Rose, "Amason's Jeff Bezos Looks To The Future," *CBS*, December 1, 2013, http://www.cbsnews.com/news/amazons-jeffbezos-looks-to-the-future/.

CPSIA information can be obtained
at www.ICGtesting.com
Printed in the USA
BVHW060049041118
531461BV00002B/9/P